Nanobrewery U.S.A.:

A Chronicle of America's Nanobrewery Beer Phenomena

Dan Woodske © 2012

About the Author:

Dan Woodske owns and operates his own nanobrewery the Beaver Brewing Company in Beaver Falls Pennsylvania with his beautiful wife Kimberly and his best friend Bemus, a 7 year old grey striped cat.

He has worked in politics, as a janitor, sales, marketing, and community development. Somehow all this ridiculous work experience cumulated into him opening a nanobrewery.

Dan graduated from the University of Pittsburgh with a degree in marketing.

He also has written 3 other books. *A Brewers Guide to Opening a Nanobrewery, Hop Variety Handbook,* and *Kvass: History, Health Benefits and Recipes.*

A Note From The Author:

First off, thank you very much for purchasing this book, it means a lot to me and I greatly appreciate it. "Thank you" isn't used enough today and I think it's important to say.

I wrote this book because there wasn't a day that someone walked into the brewery and said, "You must be the only nanobrewery in the country!" I'd answer that there are quite a few out there, but I really didn't know how many and after I looked around I found that no one really knew how many there were.

A great resource was actually put together by a fellow nanobrewer, Michael Hess of Hess Brewing. You can find it at the Hess Brewing blog. It provides a pretty nice list of active nanobreweries and also ones in planning across the U.S.

This got me really amped and I wanted to learn more about these places. What beers were they making? How did they distribute their beer? Where were they located? Why are they operating as a Nanobrewery?

The information was everywhere but it was scattered. There wasn't a resource that listed nanobreweries, told you what size system there were making, how much beer they were making, or any info from the actual brewers. In short, there was no tool that was out there promoting nanobreweries as an important and growing part of the brewery business.

It took me months (many of them) tracking down breweries across the U.S., hunting down the owners and getting 15-20 minutes of their time to share their story and let the rest of the country know what they are up to at their brewery.

There were however a handful of breweries that I could not come in contact with...not for a lack of effort though...between emails, phone calls, Facebook messages and even the dreaded written letter (yes, I actually mailed letters to these people) were used to try and get as much info as possible about the brewery.

In those cases I scoured the internet for people that had tried the beer or even better actually visited the brewery. Their thoughts are added when I couldn't wrestle the brewer away.

I believe this is the most complete resource chronicling nanobrewers i existence, however the list is changing, some get bigger, some close, and others pop up. If you know of any that I missed, please shoot me an email to dan@beaverbrewingcompany.com. I'd love to add it to th updated version of the book!

A few other quick notes...I list every breweries website, Facebook, an twitter pages. Not all of them have all of those, and when it says "yes' for Facebook it means they haven't claimed their page and have a craz long URL with 50 numbers and random letters...I wasn't listing them

You'll also notice that production numbers are added. These come from numbers that are reported to the Brewers Association®. They a not necessarily the actual numbers for tax purposes, sometimes they are estimates. Beer production is measures in Barrels (BBL). A barrel of beer is 31 US Gallons.

I think that's it...I hope you enjoy the book!

What is a Nanobrewery?

Truthfully there is no correct answer. The TTB (Alcohol and Tobacco Tax and Trade Bureau) does not define it and treats Budweiser™ the same way as Beaver Brewing Company...for the most part...

So I guess I can define it myself...*A Nanobrewery is a licensed brewery that brews malt beverages and operates on a brewing system of 3.5 BBL's or under.* Simple enough. I don't put a cap saying you can only produce 100 BBL's a year or less. If you put the work in to do it then fine, you are still a nano.

Is a nano really smaller than a microbrewery? Why the distinction?

Good question. Let's look at a few microbreweries compared to nano's. Everybody has probably heard of Dogfish Head Craft Brewery. They are considered a regional microbrewery. They brewed a total of 148,686 BBL's of beer in 2011. That's a lot of beer! That still amounts to only 1.25% market share in the craft beer market.

My brewery, Beaver Brewing Company brewed 40 BBL's in 2011...that's about 0.000000392% of the market share for the craft beer market...slightly different.

A few other things that make a nanobrewery a nanobrewery:

- Staff. Usually this consists of 1 brewer, sometimes 2 or 3 that rotate. They also rely heavily on volunteers. (This doesn't include wait staffs for those that operate pubs).
- Space. Some nano's operate out of sheds, some in less than 300 square feet. You could fit most nano's into the smallest fermenter at your local microbrewery.

- Distribution. You'll almost never see a nano cross state lines to distribute. Most either sell only in house or within a 25 mile region of the brewery.
- Capital. I don't have the numbers to back this up but I would say over ½ of the breweries in this book were self financed or financed with the help of friends and family...very few got a bank loan for their operations...

Why in God's name would someone operate on such a small scale?

If you are reading this book you understand that craft beer is EXPLODING. There is craft beer in bars you thought you'd never see it in. Every city has at least 5 or 6 local breweries fighting for tap spac in town.

Let's look at some numbers from the Brewers Association™ that helps show how much this is taking over. In 1980 there were a whooping 8 craft beer breweries in the US. 10 years later there was a paltry 211. Then in 2000 it jumps to 1,507. In 2010 it was up to 1,716!

The amount of BBL's of craft beer has increased EVERY YEAR SINCE 1969. In 2000 there were 5,307,057 BBL's of craft beer sold...in 2010 that number was 9,951,956...a 53.3% increase!

Again we are talking millions of BBL's and these nano's are pumping out 10 – 100 BBL's a year so why are they even bothering?

As you'll see many of the brewers in the book will mention that they want to go big...just not right now. It's a great way to crack into the market and essentially get paid for market testing your product.

Going small also allows brewers to test crazy experimental beers that no one else will make because if it doesn't work there isn't a few thousand gallons of beer you have to dump. I am sure most large breweries would never make Kvass, but I do 12 months a year...why? Because I can. It tastes good and customers always want it.

It also allows you to enter the market at a low cost. If it doesn't work you're out a used car and you can keep your house.

Others do it simply because they love beer. I talked to several nanos that told me they love the hobby and work towards breaking even because they love sharing the beer with their local community.

Most people will tell you a nanobrewery can't work; the numbers won't allow it...after reading this you'll discover all these brewers and owners are either crazy and love losing money or have figured a way to make it work...

Types of Nanobrewers

After doing the book I put Nanobrewers into three categories.

1. *Having Fun Category:* This is the smallest in terms of numbers. There are a handful that don't make much beer but like sharing it with their community, they keep costs low and do it as a hobby and try to break-even.
2. *Need a side job:* In this economy a lot of people are working part-time or think they may lose their job, this is kind of a safety net job that people do in their spare time and have something to fall back onto if they need it.
3. *Testing the Waters:* This is where the vast majority of nanos reside. We want to have a 15 BBL brewpub with some distribution but we don't have the money or experience to do that. Going nano allows for a brewer to perfect the craft, save money, and provide a business case for a larger brewery.

Crazy Growth within the Nano Community

If someone walked into a nanobrewery 7 years ago they'd probably think it was some sweet ass meth lab. Today they are becoming commonplace in the beer industry.

Not until about 2008 did they really begin to pick up steam, but they are now popping up almost everywhere.

This idea of picking up steam isn't just a pipe dream, but it is backed by some numbers...I included each breweries production numbers for the last 2 years reported. It's not uncommon to see 100%+ growth in production from year to year...that's not a misprint, many nano's double their capacity very quickly, some even grow at a much faster rate than that.

And this list isn't done. According to the Brewers Association there were 915 breweries in planning in 2011, up from 513 the year before...if even 1% of those were nano's we could be seeing 9-10 more of these within the next year.

I can almost guarantee that number is larger than 1%. As soon as I started my brewery I was getting 5-10 emails a week asking how I did it, what hoops did you have to jump through, etc., etc? Instead of just taking 3-4 hours of my time with each person (and believe it or not some people expect that) I started doing consulting for future nanobrewers.

I currently do about 2-4 a month and get many more inquires than I can handle.

That led me to write my first book, *A Brewers Guide to Opening a Nanobrewery: Your $10,000 brewery consultant for $15*. Sales of that book have consistently exceeded my expectations.

So I can tell you with personal experience this is not a fad that will go away, people are getting more and more into nano's and they are becoming more and more accepted by beer drinkers.

Why all the weird beers?

Because you drink them. Nanobreweries crank out some of the most unique ales in the world, but there is always some hater out there saying that's "not real beer". I hate to inform you but some of the most popular beers at these breweries have something weird about them.

Get over it, people drink them, brewers have fun with them, they are here to stay.

Getting Bigger

You will probably notice some nano's aren't on the list...that's because they got too big! The success of dozens of nano's has led to larger production breweries across the US. If you had a brew from a nano three years ago and it's not in the book check back with them...they probably grew!

Hey, you forgot about...

You're probably the kid I grew up with that told the teacher she messed up her math in grading your paper and you got an 87, not an 88. You're right, I can almost guarantee that there is a few nano's that I missed and weren't included.

I can also bet that there were 8-10 breweries I found on the web, looked like they were nano's but didn't have sufficient info on their websites and never returned my calls/emails/letters/direct messages/etc, so I couldn't add them.

If you know of one that isn't in here, please shoot me an email dan@beaverbrewingcompany.com.

Why are you writing, you should be brewing you loser!

I love to write and share stories with people. Hundreds of people asked me about nanobreweries so I figured it was just time for me to sit down and crank another book out.

On a side note I have a killer movie script called "*Zooey*" about a 16 year old that tries to seduce her older and married neighbor. That is the best thing I ever wrote in my life, optioned it once but never came to light...I'd love to see that on screen...back to beer.

Drink Local

Everyone says "Buy Local", spend money in the community. What's better than going to a nanobrewery or a bar and drinking locally sourced beer? I can guarantee you that just about every penny you spend on that beer is staying in your community.

It's also a great way to get the local flavor for a community. You'll notice almost every nano will brew at least a few beers that are directly made for locals. Some use local ingredients; others make beers that are popular in the region. In Western PA you'll find German styles, in the Pacific Northwest hopped up beers rule, in hot weather cities easy drinking saisons are popular...whatever it is there is a local flare to nano made beer.

Onto the beer!

I dare you to find a brewer that hates their job...there isn't one. These people take a lot of pride in what they do. It's hard to take pride in cleaning high school toilets (I've been there and done...it is not satisfying), but beer really inspires people and brings out their best.

What I am asking you to do is seek these places out, if they are within striking distance of you try their beer and support the nanobrewery community. Every pint makes a difference and we will all be happy to see a new face!

192 Brewing Company

Address: 7324 NE 175th S
              Kenmore, WA 98028
Website: www.192brewing.com
Twitter: N/A
Facebook: www.facebook.com/192brewing

2010 Production: 50 BBL
2011 Production: 75 BBL

Brewery Hours: M-TH 4 to 10, F-S Noon to 10pm, Sun Noon to 7pm

About the Brewery:

Derek Wyckoff is the owner/brewer at 192 Brewing. I know there are tons of brew nerds out there that love to hear about systems and how people brew. You'll find it is also a story on how the brewery got its' name... "The entire brewery is a 12 x 16 shed that I built by hand with the help of friends and neighbors. It makes up 192 square feet, from which the name comes. We have a 2 barrel system, comprised of two 60 gallon steam kettles. We sparge directly from a commercial grade on demand gas water heater. The conical fermentation tanks are food grade nylon and were a very affordable option for our startup. They work great. They are also not jacketed, so temperature control comes from a heater, and cooling comes from mother nature and cool Washington weather."

They also own the *Lake Trail Taproom Presented by 192 Brewing* (that is the listed address above) and that's where you will find all of the 192 Brewing beer, and the only place you'll find it. "We just can't make the beer fast enough to keep on tap at our own taproom, so we can't support any other accounts until we expand." But if you like the beer you better get there fast.

"When we release a new keg on tap at the taproom, it doesn't last more than a day or two at the most. Good thing we have a tavern license at the site. We feature 14 tap handles currently, with a variety of Washington-only microbrews on tap"

OPENING SOON! MAY 2012

Presenting:

192

BREWING CO.
KENMORE, WA

The Lake Trail Taproom

COME ENJOY A SAMPLE, SIP ON A PINT, OR TAKE A GROWLER TO GO!

Beers:

Derek brews as fast as he can and he talked a bit about his #1 selling beer. "The Shticky Blonde is our best selling beer, lasting about 3-4 hours per keg at a festival, and about 12 hours at the Taproom. That is an unfiltered Kolsch style beer, with wild honey added from the foothills of Mt. Rainier. It has only Saaz hops, and a crisp start, with a soft finish, and lingering honey aftertaste."

He also is trying out some newer styles also. "So far our most crazy beer has been the Blitzen's Busted Nut, which was our first winter special beer for the Strange Brew Festival in Port Townsend each January. It is made with our Apple Ale recipe, and then we add ground up Cinnamon and cloves, and a whole crushed Nutmeg in the keg. Very warm and spicy to drink on a snowy day, which it typically is for that festival."

Ambacht Brewing Company

Address: 1055 NE 25th Ave, Suite N
                 Hillsboro OR 97124
Website: www.ambacht.us
Twitter: @AmbachtAle
Facebook: www.facebook.com/AmbachtAle

2010 Production: 25 BBL
2011 Production: 50 BBL

Brewery Hours: Thursday 4-6pm and Sunday 1-4pm

About the Brewery:

"At Ambacht, we believe in producing delicious Belgian-inspired ales that are balanced, flavorful and go great with food. Our products use local, organic ingredients whenever possible. Our ales are bottle or cask conditioned using natural Oregon Blackberry Honey."[1]

Ambacht bottles most of their beer and they can be found locally in anywhere between 8-10 bottle shops and bars near their brewery. They also keg some of their beer.

Another great reason to support nanobreweries…they are completely unique in an ununique way. (I know that's not a word but I like it…you're going to have to deal with it.) They focus primarily on farmhouse Belgian inspired ales, but they bottle condition their beer…with HONEY! That's right, Belgian beers with Oregon Blackberry honey.

---

[1] http://www.ambacht.us/ambacht_ales.html

Beers:

Possibly the most interesting beer in their seasonal lineup is the Ambacht Matzobraü. This one is made right after Passover with left over Matzah. Reviews call it light and filled with sweet fruits. I'd love to get my hands on one of these...One beer reviewer, Robin Harrison of Seattle Washington, tracked down a bottle in near Portland Oregon Here's the lowdown she gave...

"I enjoyed it, thought it was an unusual style, almost a hybrid, and thought I could detect the crackery flavor of matzo in the beer, which liked. I like the beer quite a bit and will certainly try anything from the brewery again."

They also offer other variations on the Farmhouse Ale including a *Dar Farmhouse Ale* that used to be a porter. All beers come in around 6.5ᶜ ABV with the exception of their Strong Golden Ale the *G++ Ale*.

The inside of the brewery is said to be very "industrial" and the brewers are friendly to those who stop in to sample some brews.

Ancient Lakes Brewing Company

Address: 21547 Road 11.2 NW
               Quincy WA, 98848
Website: www.ancientlakesbrewing.com
Twitter: N/A
Facebook: Yes

2010 Production: 50 BBL
2011 Production: 53 BBL

Brewery Hours: N/A

<u>About the Brewery</u>:

You may think that 53 barrels (1,643 gallons) of beer isn't all that much for a year's worth of production…but when you're brewing on a 10 gallon Sabco™ system that is a lot of brewing! "On brew days I do a triple batch and we get about 1 BBL a day" Says co-owner Mike Silk. But at least they have 2 brewers. "We usually switch up the brewing so we get breaks." Mike and his wife own it with his friend John and his wife.

They brew nine quote "everyday" beers. This is a nanobrewery that focuses on a few beers and works to perfect them. They exclusively brew all ales.

In true homebrewer form they distribute their beer in soda kegs. "The bars don't mind so we haven't made it up to Sanke Kegs but look to get those when we expand." They plan on moving their brewery to a larger space and getting a larger system with a tasting room.

"This size was kind of a marketing test for us to see if the demand was out there." Says Mike.

They occasionally bottle their beers but most everything is put into kegs and doesn't last very long. "Usually there is an empty spot and the bar is waiting for our keg when we make a delivery."

Beers:

They have nine beers but the local favorite is the I-90 Pale Ale which is pictured.

The beer that is most sought after of theirs is a seasonal called *Tribulation*. It is a barley wine that

has been called "the best barley wine I have ever had" by one review.

Other regular offers include the *Fossilhead* (Hefeweizen), *Silk* (American Pale Ale), and *Quincy Gold* (Blonde Ale that is usually their best seller) that is named after the town the brewery is located.

Mike tells me they don't do too many experimental ales, "Our craziest beer out is our summer seasonal which is the Quincy Gold and we add real cherries to the fermenter."

They take a lot of pride in their beer. "We offer fine handcrafted ales that are non-filtered and carry a unique, clear, and balanced taste."

Bat Creek Brewery

Address: 4 W. Main
                  Bowling Green, MO
Website: www.batcreekbrewery.com
Twitter: @BatCreek
Facebook: www.facebook.com/batcreek

2010 Production: 35 BBL
2011 Production: 40 BBL

Brewery Hours: None

About the Brewery:

The brewery is owned by Jeremy
Gilbert and Ryan and Heather Daffron.
"We started this brewery because we are
passionate about beer." Says head brewer Jeremy Gilbert. They run a
1.5 BBL system and produce all ales.

"We take great pride in the beer; it is tested several times before we
release each new batch to the public."

"We currently don't sell on site but you can find us all around the
Bowling Green area." They sell their beer in kegs and in 22 oz. bottles.

They run the brewery out of a machine shed but have plans to make a
larger brewery down the line. "We would really like to expand within
the next year or two."

Ryan and Jeremy were avid homebrewers before opening the brewery
and figured they loved it so much they thought they should go forward
and start a licensed brewery. Within a year they bought a machine
shed, equipment, and were selling their beer locally.

<u>Beers:</u>

They have one of the coolest stories for a beer I have ever heard. The *Pike County Pale Ale* is made with Wild Missouri Hops...you have no idea how rare wild hops are.

Jeremy told me "I found them one day and said to myself that we needed to try these in a beer." They have a unique peppery and citrus flavor and aroma. "I really can't say they are like any other hop, truly unique."

However the best seller is the *Machine Shed Stout*, which has roasted and chocolate malts that help balance out the sweetness.

"We also make an *Imperial Machine Shed Stout* that was aged in bourbon soaked oak." It was over 10% ABV and made with a hint of smoke malt. Jeremy said it was a fast seller and well received when it was released.

Beaver Brewing Company

Address: 2029 15th Street
                 Beaver Falls PA 15010
Website: www.beaverbrewingcompany.com
Twitter: @beaverbrewing
Facebook: www.facebook.com/beaverbrewingcompany

2010 Production: 1   BBL
2011 Production: 40 BBL

Brewery Hours: First Friday 6 to 8pm and First Saturday 11am to 2pm
of each month.

About the Brewery:

Hard to interview myself but here I go…Dan Woodske opened the
Beaver Brewing Company with a 1.5 Barrel system. "I found myself
driving 45 minutes in every direction to go to a brewery and nothing
was else was close, I said to myself, if one was in the middle of all this
then maybe people would come?" So far the brewery has far exceeded
Dan's expectations. "I am making some unique stuff that I thought was
really underserved in the region so it was a risk, but it is paying off."

Hopefully you will read this, check out the Beaver Brewing website
and find that they are now operating a brewpub. "That is the goal, I
already own the building, now it is a matter of zoning and licensing."

Beaver Brewing is found throughout Beaver County but most of the
beer is sold on site in Growlers and the occasional bottle. "I found that
the beer was going so quickly at bars I was constantly making
deliveries and not making beer, I really geared everything towards
getting people to come into the brewery."

The brewery almost serves as a test lab. "I try to make some really
strange styles so the brewery is a great testing ground. I force you to

try everything on tap (8-12 beers) and you can tell me what you liked and what you didn't. its great info for me moving forward."

Beers:

"I love doing styles that people have never had." For most breweries these are a saison or an imperial stout, at Beaver Brewing those odd styles are the Kvass and the Roggenbier. "A Roggenbier is pretty much a Hefeweizen, but instead of wheat you add rye. I made it as a one off but people liked it so much I now rotate in about every other month."

The *Kvass* is also a rare bird, currently his brewery is the only place in the United States you can find a kvass brewed 12 months a year. "It's made with Bread, Lemons, and Raisins...I call it the health drink of the 10th century Russian peasant." The beer also comes in at 1.5% ABV...not 10.5...1.5.

Other than that you can try the *Chamomile Wheat, Basil (Amber Ale), The Ryeing Game. I.Porter.A,* or the popular seasonal the *Pecan Pie Nut Brown* brewed with 5 pounds of crushed pecans in each batch.

"I also like trying hops people aren't accustomed too." That would include the *Nelson Sauvin Pale Ale,* the *Sorachi Ace,* and the *Citra W Hopped Ale.* "Variety is the spice of life and tasting another Cascade/Columbus hopped beer can get your palate tired over time, you need to change it up," says Dan.

He also takes requests for beers too, "To date I have actually made 4 beers from peoples suggestions, this should be fun and listening to customers keeps it fresh."

The Beer Diviner

Address: 241 Bly Hollow Road
                  Cherry Plain, NY 12040
Website: www.thebeerdiviner.com
Twitter: N/A
Facebook: www.facebook.com/thebeerdiviner

2010 Production: N/A
2011 Production: N/A

Brewery Hours: None as of yet

<u>About the Brewery:</u>

If I wasn't upgrading my fermenters I would have never have known about this brewery. Dr. Jonathan Post picked up some of my old fermenters and told me about his beer.

"I had been homebrewing for years and when I lost my job as an English Professor I figured it was time to start working for myself."

Jonathan got licensed in 2012 and within a few months bumped up from a 1/3 BBL system to a 2 BBL. "I can't even come close to meeting demand for the beer."

He bottles all of it in 22's but is looking forward to possibly putting some on draft. "It is something I'd like to do, but the bottles sell so quickly that I can't see it happening soon." You can buy all of his beer around the Cherry Plain area of New York, but he does have plans to get the beer into areas further out.

While he told me he may get larger at some point, he likes the small batch feel that a nano brings "It seems to me that really small batch beers are better than bigger ones; there's some kind of manufactured, assembly-line taste even with good microbrews, but maybe that's all in my head."

Beers:

Jonathan does make something that is truly unique and may be one of the only nano's (and only breweries for that matter) that produces a Gruit Ale.

"It's something I've been experimenting with for ten years, ever since a friend sent me Stephen Buhner's book on sacred herbal beers. My goal has been not to get too much of a herby/lemonady taste, but at the

same time retain the unusual floral bouquet. Now the only herbs I put in are the artemisias, yarrow and wormwood, in the mash, in the boil and in the primary. I also finally discovered that grains of paradise work very well in gruit; in fact, I wonder if back in the middle ages they discovered the same thing."

If you have never had a gruit, take some thought into what he has to say about the ancient ale... "If I wasn't drinking all kinds of beer, because after all I'm a brewer and a brewer needs to do that, I would drink gruit all the time. It doesn't make me drowsy like hopped beer and I tend not to drink as much – which is a good thing because most of my beers are over 8% alcohol. With the gruit you definitely don't notice the alcohol until...yeah, that's what I'm talking about!"

He also puts out a Coffee Oatmeal Stout, a Pale Ale, and a Red Ale.

Benny Brew Co. @ Marty's Blue Room

Address: 100 Old Newport St.
             Naticoke, PA 18634
Website: www.martysblueroom.com
Twitter: N/A
Facebook: Yes

2010 Production: 20 BBL
2011 Production: 45 BBL

Brewery Hours: Tuesday – Saturday 5pm - 10:30pm

About the Brewery:

The brewery is located in the back of Marty's Blue Room but you will find Benny's beer in about 10 local locations. You can get the beer in bottles but mostly you will find it on draft somewhere.

"The beer is the most fresh beer around." Says Ben about his beer.

Like many other nanobrewers he brews on the ½ BBL Sabco System, but is looking to double that this year. The owner of Marty's Blue Room said they need a bigger system "We can't keep up with the demand we have right now."

Ben Schonfeld says he was a homebrewer before but wanted to "make beer with a flavor no one else had in the industry."

Beers:

So far Ben is living up to that. His *Hopenstein IPA* is receiving some great reviews online. "It's my number one seller, very popular right now." You can find it on draft and in 22 oz. bombers.

He also puts out an Oatmeal Stout, an Amber Lager, and a Belgian Wit.

Bier Brewery and Taproom

Address: 5133 East 65th Street
              Indianapolis IN, 46220
Website: www.bierbrewery.com
Twitter: N/A
Facebook: Yes

2010 Production: 5 BBL
2011 Production: 460 BBL

Brewery Hours: W – F 3pm to 7pm, Sat 1pm to 7 pm, Sun 1pm to 4pr

About the Brewery:

Darren Connor has been in the beer business since he was in college. He started at Bloomington Brewing Company and brewed there for three years, from there he moved to a homebrew shop for the next 10 years.

He now runs a 1.25 BBL system at his brewery and more than likely h is brewing right now...he pumped out 460 BBL's in 2011 and is lookin to top that again. "Pretty much I am brewing 80+ hours a week." Darren told me when he had a few minutes to write an email.

Regulars at the brewery are always amazed at how much beer is on ta (for growlers only), on each visit. "People always think it's easy and never believe me when I say how much time I have to put in. So now when people ask I just say it's extremely easy to run a nano and the beer brews and sells itself and I work only 20 hours a week."

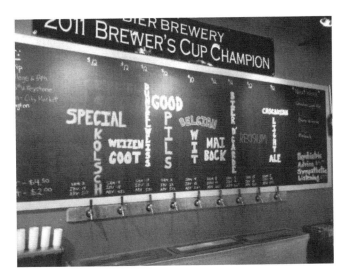

Bier Brewery usually has 9 beers on tap in house and they are different unique craft beers. To date he has made 58 different beers…he's only been open for 2 years!

Available beers for Growler Fills are listed on a huge chalkboard in the brewery and there is always something new on tap. Since they go through about 400 – 500 growlers a week there is always space freeing up for whatever is next in the lineup.

Beers:

Again, 58 different beers in fewer than two years is incredible. All the hard work put in at the brewery is allowing beer drinkers to reap the benefits.

One of the higher rated beers among the beer community is the *PDG Pale* which many people say is one of the best American Pale Ales on the market. Another winner is their *Cream Ale*.

The best thing about the brewery is that if there wasn't anything you had to have on tap that week. You can rest assured there will be something new on tap next week.

Black Husky Brewing Company

Address: W5159 Steffen Lane
Website: Pembine, WI 54156
Twitter: N/A
Facebook: Yes

2010 Production: 37 BBL
2011 Production: 71 BBL

Brewery Hours: Special Occasions

About the Brewery:

Another family owned Nanobrewery, Tim and Toni Eichinger own and operate the 4 BBL brewery which also has a Husky Dog Kennel on the property. This is their third system…they started with .5 BBL's then quickly jumped to 1.5 BBL.

"Howler", a black husky, is the unofficial mascot for the brewery. This is helpful to know because you'll notice a Black Husky beer label anytime you'd se one, "They have one of the dogs from the kennel pictured on each label." Says Tim.

"The brewery is in a small hand crafted log cabin about 6 miles off the main road. We live in a log cabin on a lake with sled dogs - hence the name Black Husky Brewing. Each of our beers is named after one of our sled dogs"

The couple started the nano because they didn't want to be "depending on another employers whims. We loved brewing so this just seemed like a logical choice for us to start a business."

They don't offer onsite consumption as of yet, "We are really small and in a remote area so not right now," says Tim about serving on site.

However you will find them in bars throughout the region as they make regular deliveries. They also keep an up to date list of everyone that has them on tap listed on their website.

Beers:

When your brewery is in a log cabin it only makes sense to me that your brew a beer with locally harvested Spruce Tips. That's what you get in the Double IPA *Sproose Joose II IPA*. It has a cult following throughout the region and is one of their best selling beers.

"There have been several accounts when I first called on them they knew about us because of the Sproose Joose. One of our largest accounts got a sample from a beer distributor even though we self-distribute" Says Tim about the Sproose.

After that they offer plenty of other beers and even some one-offs for their anniversary plus some other special releases like their *Twelve Dog Imperial Stout*.

Blackrocks Brewery

Address: 424 N. 3ʳᵈ Street
                Marquette MI, 49855
Website: www.blackrocksbrewery.com
Twitter: @BlackRocksBrew
Facebook: Yes

2010 Production: 4 BBL
2011 Production: 240 BBL

Brewery Hours: W-F 5 to 10 PM, SAT 12 – 10 PM, SUN 5 to 10 PM

<u>About the Brewery:</u>

When you are a nano and you have 4,900+ "Likes" on Facebook® you are doing something right. Check out how their production…240 BBL's!

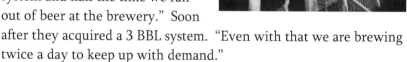

Co-Founders David Manson & Andy Langlois figured out pretty quick they needed to grow. David told me "We started with a 1 BBL system and half the time we ran out of beer at the brewery." Soon after they acquired a 3 BBL system. "Even with that we are brewing twice a day to keep up with demand."

They have a very cool "quaint historical house" in which the brewery is located. "People love the vibe of the place"

I asked why they started as a nano and how are they handling this success? "We are brewing non-stop. We always wanted to bootstrap this business but we never really thought it would take off immediately. There wasn't anything like this in the area so we had no idea how people would receive it."

"We also wanted to offer a nice variety of beers covering different styles and constantly changing them. Having a small system gave us that freedom."

You can try any of those beers on site in the tasting room. They offer pints as well as growler fills. They currently do not bottle.

His advice to future nanobrewers is "You got to love brewing. You might be doing it 12 hours a day 5 days a week if you are successful."

Beers:

To say they have a full lineup would be a disservice. "There is always something new at the brewery." While they offer many of the main stay traditional craft brews, they also like to experiment.

Take their *Chipotle Stout.* "I like to say we experiment with beer so you can let your taste buds experiment as well."

They also offer a *Lavender Honey Wheat* that goes down "very easy" but packs a punch with 7% ABV.

"Everyone at the brewery loves the pale ales but they really appreciate the variety we offer." Check out their updated beer list on their website, it is constantly changing with their newest varieties.

When I spoke with David he said they are working on one of their most experimental beers to date... *The Blackberry Sour Porter* aged in Whiskey Barrels..."This one has us excited."

When asked about what he likes most at the brewery David said, "I love when we get that guy that comes in and says 'I only drink (insert macrobrewed beer here)'. Then in 3 months he comes in and says 'I'll have your newest IPA'. That is the fun part."

Blind Bat Brewery

Address: Centerport, NY 11721
Website: www.blindbatbrewery.com
Twitter: @BlindBatBrewer
Facebook: Yes

2010 Production: 60 BBL
2011 Production: 80 BBL

Brewery Hours: None

About the Brewery:

Really glad I got a chance to chat with Paul Dlugokencky. When I saw he was making wood-smoked beers at his 3 BBL nano in New York I had to learn more. This was maybe the coolest idea I have ever heard of.

"Can't remember when I first heard about smoked beers, but it certainly intrigued me! The first smoked beer I tried brewing was when I was home brewing - what became the *Hellsmoke Porter* - in 2006, when I transitioned from extract to all-grain brewing. I played a lot with the percentage of the grain bill to be smoked, how long to smoke, etc., Paul went on to say, "I continued to tweak the recipe, the percentage kept creeping up from the low 20% range up to 30%. For a 3 BBL batch, that's 70 pounds of pale ale."

Truly a cool idea as far as I am concerned. He still works a full-time job but finds time to distribute his beers (he self distributes) throughout his region in New York. He self distributes his bottles, but has no on site sales. He is looking for bigger space so he can have onsite sales in the near future.

I love his thoughts on this question…Why Should Someone Be Drinking Your Beer? "Someone should drink my beer if they are drawn to it. I am a big believer that whatever someone enjoys is the right beer for them, and not every beer is for everyone." Couldn't agree more Paul.

Paul also went into why he went nano, "Starting real small and part-time made sense for me for a couple of reasons. First, I could not afford to go bigger when I wanted to start the brewery. Second, I believed it would be a good way to test out how the local marketplace would respond to the beers I'm interested in brewing -- which coincides with the beers I want to drink. I enjoy a hoppy IPA as much as the next person, but there are a lot of other beers that I want to explore."

Kielbasa not required.

Polish-Style Oak-Smoked Wheat Ale

Beers:

After you read a bit about the beer you will at the very least be intrigued, others may jump in the car on a beer search, "I smoke barley or wheat over a variety of woods at the brewery, depending on the beer. For my Hellsmoke Porter, I smoke English Pale Malt over a combination of Apple and Alder wood."

This book is packed with off-the-wall beers, but this one is crazy simply for the amount of wheat in it, unheard of in the brewing world.

"For *Vlad the Inhaler* (a recreation of the old Polish style called Grodziskie, a very smoky beer) I smoke wheat over oak. For Vlad, 100% of the wheat used in the mash is smoked, and 99% of the grist for the Vlad is Wheat. 1% Munich malt is added to satisfy Federal regulations that beer offered for sale must contain barley. I smoke the Munich malt over oak as well.

Other beers include the *Long Island Potato Stout™* that is "twice mashed", *The Long Island Oyster Stout* made with real Long Island Oysters, and the *Honey & Basil Ale* (seriously, I didn't steal that one, mine doesn't have honey ☺).

He also pumps out some new seasonal from time to time so check the website for the latest news.

Blind Pig Brewery

Address: 120 N Neil Street
                 Champaign, IL 61820
Website: www.blindpigbrewery.com
Twitter: @BlindPigBrewPub
Facebook: Yes

2010 Production: 10 BBL
2011 Production: 200 BBL

Brewery Hours: See website

About the Brewery:

I wasn't able to track down the owners for this one but I was able to track down one of their biggest fans, Justin Pogue from Champagne. "I've actually been back there about ten thousand times"

His description was so perfect I am adding everything he told me. "An important thing to note regarding the Blind Pig is that there are actually two of them about a block away from one another: The Blind Pig (often nicknamed "the Big Pig" by locals), and The Blind Pig Brewery (affectionately referred to as the Piglet). Both are staffed by friendly and knowledgeable bartenders.

The Blind Pig has the more expansive tap selection, is typically a bit more crowded on the weekends, and does not actually serve any of the Blind Pig brews.

The Brewery is about a two minute walk from there, and is the place to go if you'd like to sample the in-house-brewed beers. They typically have 2-4 in-house beers on tap in addition to a handful of rotating guest taps. The Brewery is usually a quieter, more relaxed atmosphere.

A final important note for travelers to the area is that the Blind Pig does not offer growler fills due to the brewery's lower capacity and the high local demand for their brews." Thanks Justin, maybe you should write a book!

I also got some feedback from another traveler, here's what he had to say, "I appreciate the fact that they are not your typical small-town brewery with only average offerings of blonde ale, brown ale, IPA and light lager. They will brew an Imperial Stout, then an American Pale Ale and a Barleywine for the winter."

I'd also like to add that many other reviewers have the same thing to say about the place, generally a cool place to grab a solid craft beer and they appreciate the different beers that pop up on tap.

Beers:

Here is a look at what their Summer Beer Menu churns out:

Blind Pig Maibok: A traditional German Style Pale Bock. It is unfiltered and lagered for 6 weeks.

Blind Pig Apricot Wheat: Brewed with 100 pounds of Michigan Apricots.

Blind Pig American Dark Ale: They don't call it a Cascadian or a Black IPA, they prefer Dark Ale. They add some nice roasty malts to the mix.

Blue Heron Brewing

Address: 2214 HWY 68
              Embudo, NM
Website: www.blueheronbrews.com
Twitter: N/A
Facebook: Yes

2010 Production: 5 BBL
2011 Production: 50 BBL

Brewery Hours: S-TU 12pm to 6pm   W-SAT 10am to 8pm

About the Brewery:

Blue Heron Brewing is truly a family
business, "It is my husband Scott
Hennelly, my brother Joshua Johnson,
and I, (Kristin Hennelly), that started the
brewery with a lot of hard work. Joshua
and I grew up making wine in our family's winery. An old family
friend Brandon Santos helps us brew the beer. We have three young
children who are under toe most of the time, hopefully future
brewers."

They serve all their beer on site. You can hang out and enjoy a pint on
their patio or you can take a 22 oz bottle or a growler to enjoy at home.

Kristen tells me that they are hoping to open a 7 BBL brewery at some
point, but for now they are enjoying their 3 BBL system. "We are a
tiny family owned and operated brewery. My three kids are always
running around the place. Our beer has a unique style due to our
delicious water and the grain bills that we use. This makes for a well
balanced full bodied beer."

And if you are dreaming of opening a brewery but think the
equipment may be too much to buy…build your own!

"Scott (my husband) is a biochemist. He is quite an engineer as well as a brewmaster. He made alot of our brewing equipment and hand-made my beautiful growler filler/bottler. Creating first class, high-quality equipment is his specialty."

Beers:

"Our *La Llorona Scottish Ale* is probably our most popular beer. It is a dark, malty ale with a chocolate finish," says Kristen about their best seller.

They also make stouts, red ales and even a few of the hoppier beers, "Our IPAs and Pale ale are also quite popular."

But they are always looking to try something new at the brewery. "Right now we are playing with wheat beers a little and trying different yeast."

Brewers Union Local 180

Address: 48329 E. 1ˢᵗ Street
              Oakridge, OR 97463
Website: www.brewersunion.com
Twitter: N/A
Facebook: www.facebook.com/brewersunion

2010 Production: 104 BBL
2011 Production: 114 BBL

Brewery Hours: SU – W 12 to 9, TH – SA 12 to 10 pm

About the Brewery:

Ted Sobel is the owner and brewer at his family owned Brewers Union Public house in Oregon. If you want "Real Ale" this is one of the few in the country that offer it. All his beer is also served on cask.

So what is "Real Cask Ale"? "I have to describe this to almost everyone that comes in the brewery." Says Ted about his beer. "Real Ale means

that no CO2 is added, the secondary fermentation takes place right in the cask. We also hand pump the beer to your glass." The beer is also served at cellar temperatures which range in between 50 – 55 degree Fahrenheit. "No the beer isn't warm, that is what it is supposed to be like."

Ted did his beer training in England, that's why you'll see all the casks. You'll also notice the vibe inside the bar is very much from across the pond. "I wanted to bring the public house from England to the US not just in beer, but in style. Too many places have no warmth or feel to them. You'll always get that feeling here, some people hang out all day at the pub and we encourage that."

They are brewing frequently at the Public House using only a 2.8 BBL system for their beers.

99% of the beer is served on site mostly in pints but they will fill up a growler here and there. "The beer is best consumed right from the cask but we do fill growlers."

They also offer a full menu of some of the best food in town. So come hungry as well as thirsty.

I had to ask about the name, where did it come from? Are you a Union workplace? "No, we are family owned. "Union" is about the unity of the place, it's a great place to meet. "Local" means just that, we are all locals here. "180" stands for the 180 degree turnaround this place is from anywhere else you have ever been too in the states."

Beers:

We know the uniqueness about them being all cask real ales, but here is a little rundown of what to expect there.

"We focus mostly on traditional English Ales, but that doesn't mean we don't put a west coast edge to them every once in awhile." Being in the Pacific Northwest you know there has to be some hoppy beers in there and he does have those, but he also offers several English Milds and Bitters. "We are constantly rotating new beers on tap, but you'll always see some traditional English Ales on the board."

There are plenty of one-off beers made there so check their website frequently for the latest arrival.

If you think lowly carbonated beer may not be your thing the Brewer Union also offers a few "guest" beers on tap with CO_2 pumping them in.

Chappell Brewery

Address: 5024 Highway 140
                 Mariposa CA, 95338
Website: N/A
Twitter: N/A
Facebook: Yes

2010 Production: 8 BBL
2011 Production: 3 BBL

Brewery Hours: TH – SAT 3 to 6 pm

About the Brewery:

Scott Chappell is the owner/operator of this brewery and it is truly a NANO brewery churning out less than 10 bbl's of beer each year it has been open.

Scott runs a 10 gallon system and a larger 1 BBL system at the brewery. "I wanted to start really small and test the waters, see what beers I made were popular and which ones weren't then see if I should go bigger."

Scott was a homebrewer serving his beers for free at wine tastings in the area for a few years, and then something started to happen, "People started asking if they could buy it. I figured that was a sign I needed to start a nano and see if I could take it somewhere."

Everything Scott makes goes into bottles, "It's just easier that way." You will only find them at the brewery…for now. "In 2013 I want to start making a bit more and getting some more out to a few local bars and see how the sales go there. If it works out well I think I will have to start making some more." Here's to it working out for Scott and getting more nano-brewed beer in the market.

Beers:

"I am always changing it up…trying new styles of beer seeing what people like most." Scott also says that the best feedback has come from his Nut Brown Ale which he says always gets the response of 'very drinkable'.

He doesn't do any experimental beers. "I stick to the main styles of beer." Along with the Nut Brown he makes Red Ale and an English Brown made with Hazelnut.

Cocoa Beach Brewing Company

Address: 150 N Atlantic Ave
                Cocoa Beach, FL 32931
Website: www.cocoabeachbrewingcompany.com
Twitter: @CocoaBeachBrew
Facebook: Yes

2010 Production: 150 BBL
2011 Production: 250 BBL

Brewery Hours: T-TH 1 to 9pm, F-SA 1pm to 11pm

<u>About the Brewery:</u>

Cocoa Beach operates a 1.5 BBL system but has
some nice fermentation space with a total of 13
BBL's worth on site so they can crank out a ton of
beer. They also have a true rare item for
nanobreweries…a bottling machine!

They have a tasting room on site with 2 Cocoa Beach taps and 2 guest
taps. "It has a pretty nice vibe in there," says Peter L. a local in Cocoa
Beach. "It almost feels like you are sitting in your living room at a
party when drinking in there."

They also bottle their beer and distribute throughout the region.

<u>Beers:</u>

TWELVE ADDITIONS OF FUGGLE HOPS…that immediately caught
my eye. That's what goes into the *Not Just Another Oatmeal Stout*. It
is one of their more popular beers at the brewery according to Peter
and he tells me it has a huge hop profile.

Another favorite with the tourists is the *Key Lime Cerveza*. It is made
with a healthy amount of Pilsner malts and real Key West Limes.

Corcoran Brewing Company

Address: 14635 Corkys Farm Lane
                     Waterford, VA 20197
Website: www.corcoranbrewing.com
Twitter: @CorcoranBrew
Facebook: www.facebook.com/CorcoranBrewing

2010 Production: N/A
2011 Production: 12 BBL

Brewery Hours: Saturdays 12am – 5pm

<u>About the Brewery</u>:

This is Virginia's first winery/brewery. They operate a 1 BBL system on site.

They also have a tasting room where you can sample flights of what they have on tap, as well as fill a growler of your favorite beer.

Their beer is all served on site in their taproom. Unfortunately this is one of the breweries I couldn't run down and reviews of the place are scare.

<u>Beers</u>:

They rotate their beers regularly and are making some interesting ales. Their most unique beer is probably the *Padawan Pumpkin*. Their website describes the Jedi themed beer. "In the Jedi religion, a "Padawan" is a pupil who is being trained by a Jedi Knight. Our brewer's padawan, aka his then five year old son, helped him grow the first pumpkins and crush the grain for the first version of this recipe We use lots of pumpkins from local farms (Wegemeyer and Great Country Farms), local honey, and traditional pumpkin pie spices to create this seasonal favorite. Amber to brown in color, it has all of the flavors of fall."

Cutters Brewing Company

Address: 1927 S Curry Pike
                Bloomington IN
Website: www.cuttersbrewing.com
Twitter: @CuttersBrewing
Facebook: www.facebook.com/cuttersbrewingcompany

2010 Production: N/A
2011 Production: N/A

Brewery Hours: Saturday 12 – 8pm

About the Brewery:

Monte Speicher (Co-Founder) tells me how they started Cutters Brewing. "We started out as home brewers and decided to take the plunge. We love making quality hand crafted beer and sharing it with those who appreciate the hard work that goes into making a great product.

They operate their 3 BBL brewery in Bloomington Indiana. "We are not full-time yet, we still have full-time jobs so we don't have regular brewery hours yet." They don't sell beer at the brewery, but that may change as they plan on doing a 30 BBL brewery in the future.

With that said it still isn't hard to find their beer, "We sell our beer in 22 oz bombers at local liquor stores and grocery stores. We are on tap at 10-15 bars and restaurants in Central and Southern Indiana."

They take a lot of pride in what they do and how they do it. "We are completely owner and volunteer run. We hand craft, hand bottle/keg, hand label and cap, etc. We work hard to make a quality product and celebrate the hard working Hoosiers that appreciate a quality craft beer."

He does share some wise words for future Nanobrewers... "Innovation is the key. Look for creative ways to build or modify equipment...We made a counter pressure filler, created a cold room for temp controlled fermentation, etc."

Beers:

Monte told me their most experimental beer is also the most popular, "Empire Stout is by far our most "special" beer. It has been a big hit with customers and reviewers alike. We are releasing a batch that aged in a heaven hill bourbon barrel this year."

Drewsefs a user on *beeradvocate.com ™* gave me a rundown of cutters... "The monon wheat was a light, summery ale which was bought off the shelf at a corner liquor store in Bloomington. Despite it humble origins, this wheat ale was one to impress, although there was nothing incredible that stuck out about it, it is an ale anyone would have a safe bet of trying next time they were near Indiana University.

Cutter had always been a local brewery that piqued the interest of people around town, and the beer with most acclaim to the Bloomington population would be the Half-Court IPA (a single IPA) which had a citrusy taste. When trying it, anyone would cast it aside as another IPA. But, there is a mouthfeel afterwards which ignites your taste buds into a frenzy of indescribable puckering and refreshing taste."

Monte tells me they plan on many more beers down the line so keep your eyes peeled!

Dirty Bucket Brewing Company

Address: 19151 144th Ave NE
                 Woodinville WA, 98072
Website: www.dirtybucketbrewery.com
Twitter: @TheDirtyBucket
Facebook: Yes

2010 Production: N/A
2011 Production: N/A

Brewery Hours: Friday 4-9pm, Saturday noon-7pm, Sunday noon-5pm

About the Brewery:

Shout "Hey, Acord" into the brewery and one of the three owner/operators will turn their heads. Steve, Chris, (co-founders), and Sharon Acord run the ½ BBL nano-brewery in Washington.

Steve says they choose the nano route "because we wanted to stay small and not jump right into a production brewery."

The brothers got their inspiration from another former nano-brewer who isn't doing too bad right now, "My brother and I pay homage to our "Home Brewing" roots with our name. Dirty Bucket Brewery is more than a name for our company it is a piece of our history and where we came from in the brewing community. Our favorite quote from Sam Calagione, CEO and Founder of Dogfish Head Brewery is now painted on our brewery wall *"Starting Small and Dreaming Big"*. It reminds us daily of where we were and where we are going."

They plan on moving into a production sized facility down the road, but for now you can stop in the brewery and grab a pint of your favorite Dirty Bucket brew. They also do four glass flights and growlers to go. They serve ALMOST all of the beer at the brewery. They also make deliveries to a handful of bars in the area.

Beers:

"Our most popular beer is our *Filthy Hoppn' IPA*. This is the Northwest so it is always about the hops here. We live in the land of hop heads and we have to have a beer that satisfies their need for the little green gem. "Says Steve about their best seller.

Probably their most unique beer is the *Full Nelson Indian Black Ale* made with Nelson Sauvin Hops. If you have ever had a beer with that hop you are in for a treat, seeing them in a black ale is truly a rare find. This is the first I have ever seen of this and wish this place wasn't a few thousand miles from me.

They also offer a few other pales, an oatmeal stout and an Irish Red. All their beers are very "sessionable" and almost all come in under 7% ABV.

Dunbar Brewing Company

Address: 22720 El Camino Real, Ste A
             Santa Margarita, California, 93453
Website: n/a
Twitter: @dunbarbrewing
Facebook: www.facebook.com/dunbar.brewing

2010 Production: 30 BBL
2011 Production: 35 BBL

Brewery Hours: Sat-Sun Noon to 8pm

About the Brewery:

Thankfully a former local to the area, Nick Lovgren, was able to get me some information on the vibe at the brewery. "It's a tight fit inside which gives it a very at home friendly feel. Every day seems to be a good day at Dunbar Brewing. Excellent guest taps, British-inspired house brews, and monthly beer dinners keep the locals coming back night after night. Your initial impression might leave you feeling like the new kid at school, but these guys warm up quickly and are VERY generous!"

They operate a 3 BBL system and sell all their beers in house on draft, no bottles.

They have some very tempting beer dinners there with some very good beer food.

Beers:

They usually have 2-4 house brews on tap at the pub and 1-2 guest taps. Their more popular brews are their *Scottish Heavy* and *Brown Porter*. Unfortunately I couldn't track down the brewers for this place and they don't list much info on the net.

DUO Brewing

Address: Puyallup, WA 98372
Website: www.duobrewing.com
Twitter: @duobrewing
Facebook: www.facebook.com/duobrewingllc

2010 Production: N/A
2011 Production: 3 BBL

Brewery Hours: None

<u>About the Brewery:</u>

Dan O'Leary is brewing beer in Washington so I was sure when I

talked to him he would tell me his main beer was some hoppy I.P.A…that was not the case…

"We don't even make an I.P.A. at the brewery." Says Dan about their lineup. "The Washington market is flooded with I.P.A.'s and we would have a rough time finding tap space."

Now the problem is quite the opposite. "It was tough but after that firs account we got another, then another, and it snowballed from there." DUO Brewing uses a Sabco ½ Barrel system in a detached garage in hi: backyard.

"We wanted a 10 BBL system but instead of waiting around forever fo: the money and just dreaming we said we really need to just give it a g and see where it takes us." Now Dan says they have trouble keeping up with the demand for the beer. "We figured let's do what we can with what we have and see if we have something here, we can always get bigger down the road."

Since the brewery is on his homestead property there are no on site sales, but the beer is throughout the Puyallup area. "We try to keep everything as local as possible including the ingredients." They use honey from a local beekeeper, locally roasted coffee, and their spent grain goes to a local farm. "If we are asking locals to drink our beer we need to be supporting the local economy ourselves."

They do hit some bars 30-40 minutes away from the brewery but almost everything is sold within a 15-20 minute radius of the home base.

The plans are to have a larger system and taproom down the line, but for now they are just working to get their 1st Anniversary Beer done.

Beers:

Again, truly unique to a Washington state brewery, no big hoppy I.P.A. But they make a damn good Porter, two of them actually. "The *Twin Ports Porter* is easily our best seller, but our fans favorite beer might be our *Twin Ports Coffee Porter.*"

They jam 1 pound of coffee into each sixtel they make…not batch, sixtel. That's gonna give one hell of a coffee flavor and aroma.

A summer favorite is the *Judas Kiss Belgian Style Golden Ale* brewed with local Blackberry Honey. "It was important to us that we used local honey." They add 5.5 pounds of it to every 27 gallon batch.

Dan's favorite is easily their Scotch Ale. "It's our biggest beer at 7.2% ABV and I have been working the recipe for years."

Barleywinefiend of www.beeradvocate.com™ gave me this rundown of DUO Brewing. "DUO brewing is fast becoming one of, if not the premier Nano-brewery South of Seattle. In a short amount of time, in the midst of a saturated market, DUO has been able to continually impress BJCP members, locally established brewers and beer aficionados alike."

He says this about the DUO Poles Apart Milk Stout, "Taste is immediate roastiness but not as heavy as a traditional stout ...Tasty and enough to keep me smiling and my sweet tooth satisfied."

Since the brewery is less than a year old they are planning many new beers. "We don't want to be all about one-off beers so we want a few solid ones out there and as in many places as possible at first...but we do want to do a sour ale and maybe some barrel aged beers in the future. We will definitely be keeping it fresh."

Enegren Brewing Company

Address:	680 Flinn Ave, #31
	Moorpark, CA 93021
Website:	www.enegrenbrewing.com
Twitter:	@enegrenbrewing
Facebook:	www.facebook.com/enegrenbrewing

2010 Production: None
2011 Production: N/A

Brewery Hours: W 6 to 9, F 7 to 9, SA 11am to 8pm, SU noon to 5pm

About the Brewery:

Brothers Chris and Matt Enegren and a college buddy Joe Nascenzi founded Enegren in July of 2011. The guys tell me that, "We really wanted to get into the brewing business, but didn't have a lot of money to buy a bigger brewery. We could have taken out loans and other financing, but instead we pooled all our money together and bought the biggest system we could afford (3 BBL)." And they aren't done there, "The low cost, and low risk was a great entry point into the brewing industry. We've learned a lot on the small scale that will greatly help us out when we transition to a 30bbl brewery in about 3 years."

They also welcome people into the brewery where they can sample the beer as well as take home a growler of beer. "When you come in on weekends you can watch us brew, learn about the process, and see everything in action. We love giving tours and in-depth explaining how beer is made. We find that the greater understanding someone has in understanding how beer is made, the greater appreciation they have for craft beer."

Other than in the brewery they serve their beer in local taverns throughout the area.

Beers:

They have two flagship beers. First is their *Protector.* "Protector Imperial IPA is brewed with a variety of American hops and German malt. The hops impart a citrus and spicy flavor to the beer. This is contrasted out by the German malt which adds a slightly sweet finish to the beer. Combined the two produce a well balanced yet hoppy Imperial IPA."

Next is the Valkyrie, "This is a California twist on a traditional German style Altbier. This beer is brewed with over 60% Munich Dark Malt from Germany which creates a distinct toasty, caramel and smooth taste balanced with just a hint of bitterness from American and German Noble hops."

When asked about their best selling beer it was tough, "It's a dead even tie between our IPA and altbier. The IPA is for those craft beer lovers that need hops and lots of them. The Altbier not only satisfies a craft beer drinker because of its uniqueness, but "non-beer drinkers" seem t enjoy it as well since it's malty, a bit sweet and smooth."

Epic Ales

Address: 3201 1st Ave South, Suite 104
                Seattle, WA 98134
Website: www.epicales.com
Twitter: @epicales
Facebook: Yes

2010 Production: 60 BBL
2011 Production: 80 BBL

Brewery Hours: Friday 3:30 to 8 pm and Saturday noon to 4pm

About the Brewery:

Cody Morris is the owner and brewer at this now 3 BBL brewery in Seattle. "I started with a 1 BBL brewhouse and soon found that I needed a larger one." Said Cody.

All the people I talked to for the book were passionate about it, but Cody REALLY takes pride in his brews. Each beer is made with a thought. "How will this pair with food?"

Cody wanted to get into brewing after school but couldn't find a job at a brewery so he worked at a homebrew store. "It was great experience, I got to learn about just about every grain and yeast there was and as able to talk to other brewers on a daily basis."

From there he went to a specialty food and wine shop. "I was delivering white truffles to restaurants with exquisite wine lists and possibly the most boring beer offerings ever. People were pairing great food with great wine and I thought they should be pairing it with great beer also."

EPICALES

every possibility is conceivable

Soon after Cody was bottling and brewing in his commercial space. He bottles most of the beer, but is doing more drafts. "I've just went through my 20,000 bottle...that gets a little old when you are doing it by hand." He distributes to plenty of bottle shops but soon you'll be able to drink his beer in his new brew pub.

"I teamed up with a chef that I worked with on a few beer dinners, he is phenomenal and really understands pairing." He and Cody have paired to create a very unique high end food/beer place. "This just made sense for both of us, great beer, and great food together. If you want a beer that tastes like nothing you've ever experienced before yo need to stop in."

Beers:

"I don't want to say I am doing some of the most unique ales in the region," says Cody. Well if you don't want to say it, I will.

Personally, I love what he is doing, he makes my beer look like your normal pale lager. "I've always liked to experiment and having the 1 BBL system really allowed me to do that."

One of his more experimental beers was the *Cinco Plantas*. It was brewed with Epazote. The Mexican herb has a VERY strong taste. "Pairing this one was interesting since it had such an overwhelming flavor to it. But I had a lot of fun making it."

His best seller is the Solar Trans Amplifier. "It's kinda a Wit meets Saison with Sake Yeast type of beer." He pairs it with Fish and Salad.

There is always something unique offered there, "We did a Beet Down beer which was made with Beets and a Wild Fermentation. It was sour and poured a bright purple color, very cool." He and his chef ended up making a delicious tempura batter that went on Halibut steaks from the beer.

He also does a coffee like beer called the OTTO-Optimizer which is very popular. "It has some very strong coffee in it and types of coffee flavors people are not used to."

If you are into beer dinners, a stop at Epic Ales is a must.

Exit 6 Brewery

Address: 5055 Hwy N
                  Cottleville MO 63385
Website: www.exit6brewery.com
Twitter: @Exit6Brewery
Facebook: www.facebook.com/exit6

2010 Production: N/A
2011 Production: N/A

Brewery Hours: M-S 4pm to 1:30am Sunday 5pm to Midnight

About the Brewery:

Jeff's story isn't to different than many others the last couple years, his IT job was outsourced and he was looking for work, "I've always wanted to open the bar so I took my 401(k) and decided I need to give this a go." And it is going pretty well.

"Right now I can't keep anything I make on tap very long," says Jeff. II started with a 22 gallon system in the brewery which is about 30 minutes outside of St. Louis, but soon found that wouldn't be enough He bumped up to a 1.5 BBL system in only a few months. "It's still hard to keep up with demand even though we have 25 beers on tap at all times. We opened less than a year ago and we keep on growing." Besides the Exit 6 beer you will find 20 other craft beers on tap.

Jeff says he loves running a nanobrewery but is already considering another location with a larger system. "I'd like to possibly distribute the beer down the road." But he will always run at least one nano, "If you have never been to a nanobrewery you have to go. They have the freedom to make whatever they want and will try stuff a big brewery wouldn't even think of, you really get a variety from a nano like nowhere else."

Beers:

Exit 6 has 3 flagship beers you will always find on tap. *The Vanilla Cream Ale* (which Jeff says is easily the best seller), *Ryane's Red* (An Amber named after his daughter that has 76 IBU's), and their Pale Ale.

"After that I haven't brewed one of our 2 rotating beers twice yet, we love the variety." He did mention that one will be coming back, possibly the most experimental beer he has put out, *The Raspberry Jalapeño Cream Ale*. "It had a crazy sweet/hot thing going on the people have been requesting for months, it will be coming back at some point."

Beyond that there is always something out of the ordinary on tap and well worth the trip for people getting off at Exit 6.

Fenton Winery and Brewery

Address: 1545 N. Leroy St.
Fenton, MI 48430
Website: www.fentonwinery.com
Twitter: N/A
Facebook:
www.facebook.com/FWBlounge

2010 Production: 10 BBL
2011 Production: 20 BBL

Brewery Hours: M-T 3pm to 10pm F 3 to
Midnight, SA 1 to midnight

About the Brewery:

Matt Sherrow of Fenton Winery is pumping out both beer and wine at his location in Michigan. "I started the nanobrewery primarily because of the relatively low cost of getting up & running." He is running a ½ BBL system right now.

Matt likes the nano system for the same reason dozens of the other nano's like it, "The positive for me with a nano is that I can rotate beer frequently without having a large quantity to sell before tapping a new style of beer."

They serve all their beer on site in pints "And you can always get a growler to go," says Matt. There is no distribution of the beer as of yet so you have to stop in if you want to try their ales.

Probably the most unique part of winery/brewery is the variety of drinks you can have on a visit. "We have 13 beers on tap, 3 Sodas, and 20+ wine varieties available."

Beers:

So I know what you are thinking…do they use the old wine barrels?

Matt gives us the lowdown, "As a winery, I have 3 red wines that are aged in European oak barrels prior to bottling. After I have used my barrels for about 2 years, I'll retire them from winemaking. I then brew a double batch of my Scottish Wee Heavy. Half of it goes into the wine barrel the other half gets bottle conditioned. I let the beer age a minimum of 6 months prior to kegging. We allow customers to purchase the beers and drink them side-by-side to help them understand the effects of aging the beer in old wine barrels. It adds some toffee, molasses, caramel, and sour notes."

Matt says their Wheat Beer is probably the most popular. "Other than that it is our Honey Amber (a rotating tap) or the Black IPA (a standard tap)."

They also offer a gluten-free beer, *Gluten For Punishment Cream Ale.*

Across the board they offer a wide variety of beers from higher alcohol, to session beers, malty, hoppy…just about everything your palate could desire.

Foggy Noggin Brewing

Address: 22329 53rd Ave SE
                Bothell, WA 98021
Website: www.foggynogginbrewery.com
Twitter: @fognog
Facebook: Yes

2010 Production: 1 BBL
2011 Production: 12 BBL

Brewery Hours: Most Saturdays 1-4 & the Occasional Friday

About the Brewery:

Even though I only exchanged email with Jim Jamison (Manager/Brewmaster/Owner) of the family owned Foggy Noggin I can tell he runs a great place and is a great guy. You have to be a great guy to run a family owned brewery that is located on your residential property!

Tucked away 20 miles north east of Seattle they make all of their beer on a ½ BBL System. "Visitors can bring their own food to the brewery to enjoy with our beers." (Something I personally love about nano's.)

When you visit you will find 4 beers on tap with CO_2 and they even have 2 beers on Nitro, a true rare find in the nano-brewing world. I don't know of another brewery doing less than 30 BBL's a year and having their beer on Nitro. They serve tasters, pints, and growlers on site.

He says one of his major problems is that bars want the beer all of the time. "A lot of bars want their beer on tap all of the time but we just can't do that." They rotate the bars they distribute to and drop off a keg about once every 8 to 12 weeks.

Jim is also very excited about the Seattle beer scene which consistently ranks among the best in the country, "If you want great beer your next beer expedition has to be Seattle."

Jim is also no "noob" to craft beer. Back in 1994 he started the Northwest Brew News (NWBN), a subscription based newsletter. By 1997 he had 15,000 subscribers.

In 2007 he started putting together recipes with his family and perfecting them and opening in 2010.

He says he wasn't quite ready to go full-time and that's why he started as a nano, "I wanted to share great beer throughout the community."

Beers:

Probably the most experimental beer from Foggy Noggin is the *PowderKeg*, a coffee stout that is "dry-beaned". They are looking to bottle that this year.

Now I read about beer all the time and session beers are constantly coming in and out of style according to the "pros" and gets ragged on quite a bit as not a cool style.

But don't tell that to Jim. "Our most popular beer is the *Bit O' Beaver*. It has a low ABV of 3.4% but is the ultimate session beer. It has a nice smooth malty flavor to it." Reviews back it up with almost everyone commenting on how easy it is to drink.

Their other "Flagship" beer is something you would think would be a seasonal, *The Christmas Duck*. "Everyone deserves to celebrate Christmas year-round!" Cascade, Fuggle, Willamette, and Golding hops are poured into this year-round Porter.

While they serve most of the beer on tap you will find the occasional seasonal pop into a bottle.

Hank Is Wiser Brewing

Address: 213 N Main Street
               Cheney, Kansas, 67025
Website: www.hankiswiserbrewery.com
Twitter: N/A
Facebook: http://www.facebook.com/hankiswiserbrewery

2010 Production: 50 BBL
2011 Production: 50 BBL

Brewery Hours:

Thursday 5:30 to Midnight, Friday 5:30 to 2:00 am and Saturday to 5:3 to 2:00 am

About the Brewery:

I've worked in politics, sales, marketing, and community development All this has given me a keen sense of finding out within 30 seconds if you are dealing with good people or not. With Hank it took me about 15 seconds, this is a good guy.

He runs a truly family owned bar and brewery. He used to be the brewer but gave that responsibility to his son full-time a few years ago He and his wife tend bar at their local tavern. "We're in a small town and when we started people kinda looked at us funny asking what 'craft beer' even was. We changed that pretty quickly."

All of the 50 Barrels that were brewed at the brewery were sold on sit last year and they intend on keeping it that way in the future. This is another example of a hard working brewery, they pumped out these 5 barrels with a 15 gallon Sabco™ system. "If I had one bit of advice to give to someone opening a brewery I would say buy something bigger than a 15 gallon system." He also told me he'd love one himself but doesn't have the space in the bar.

There is plenty more than the regular Hank is Wiser brews on tap. They offer 75+ other craft (some really hard to find stuff and they list most of it on their website) and macro brews at the bar and in 2013 they hope to offer a full BBQ menu with ribs and other smoked meats. Hank says they even have a vertical offering of Sam Adams® Utopia's from '03, '05. '07, and '11. "People have driven over a hundred miles to try those."

Currently they only offer the pulled pork sandwich. "People love it, but we want to offer more."

Hank was in sales for years traveling the country but when his company asked him to spend some more time on the road he rethought his career, "I figured I had to make a change and had been thinking of a brewery/bar for years, this gave me the opportunity."

He took it…and a few months later he retired at noon and had the grand opening for the bar at 3 pm that same day.

They do fill growlers there but most patrons like to sit around and grab a beer at the pub. They have bottled beer, but those are rare finds at the brewery.

"We operate a family owned bar and brewery in a small town in Kansas and it really feels like it when you walk in the door, people around here really appreciate that." Mentioned Hank when I asked him about the vibe of the place.

Beers:

Who said craft beer was expensive? $3.75 a pint? People in New York City are passing out right now. Hank offers some of the least expensive craft beer out there.

Hank says that the *Eh! Canadian Lager Style Ale* is easily the most popular beer at the brewery but people flock to the Oak Aged beers when they have them. "It seems that whenever we have the oak aged stuff it runs out almost instantly".

They have plenty of seasonals like the *Cherry Poppin' Pale Ale (a side note: I have always wanted to call a beer "Hoppin' the Cherry" but have yet to make a cherry beer...my label would also be completely tasteless, back to Hank), Honey and Oats Brown Ale* and even a Barley Wine was thrown into the mix several times over the years.

If I am ever going through "fly-over" country in Kansas this will be high on my list of stops I need to make.

Healdsburg Beer Company

Website: www.healdsburgbeerco.com
Twitter: @healdsbrew
Facebook: Yes

2010 Production: N/A
2011 Production: 80 BBL

Brewery Hours: None

About the Brewery:

Kevin McGee owns and operates the brewery in Sonoma County California, that's not a misprint…a BREWERY in Sonoma County California. "I was into some consulting for several wineries in the area and seeing that process got me into brewing my own beer." Soon after he began brewing more often and it turned into a "serious hobby".

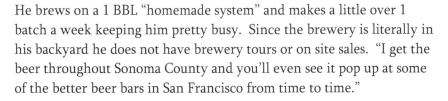

"I want to figure out the business on the small end then if I could get a handle on it, expand to a larger capacity brewery." He mentioned that would not be a 7 BBL system but something much larger to be a regional brewery. "I really want to take it to the next level if I can."

He brews on a 1 BBL "homemade system" and makes a little over 1 batch a week keeping him pretty busy. Since the brewery is literally in his backyard he does not have brewery tours or on site sales. "I get the beer throughout Sonoma County and you'll even see it pop up at some of the better beer bars in San Francisco from time to time."

Beers:

All of the Healdsburg beers are naturally carbonated, that means the yeast stays in the bottle/keg and carbonates the beer.

The brewer also recommends that they should be served in a wine glass or a goblet.

Kevin says his most popular beer that bars are always requesting is the Lytton Cask. Instead of me trying to explain it, let's see exactly what the brewer has to say about it... *"The Lytton Cask is difficult to define "This Cask found its origins in one of our winter seasonal ales and was so well received we moved it into regular production. Roughly describable as the black-sheep child of a robust porter and a foreign extra stout, The Lytton Cask is a complex ale with an intriguing depth of flavor, but remains an easy drinking pint. The Lytton Cask won a Bronze medal at the 2010 U.S. Open Beer Championship in the Porter category."*

The brewery also makes a few seasonals each year with the Golden Ale Belgian made with local honey being among the more popular.

His advice to potential nanobrewers..."Have a long-term plan, mine is expansion. Don't start without one."

Hess Brewing Company

Address: 7955 Silverton Ave.
                San Diego CA, 92126
Website: www.hessbrewing.com
Twitter: @hessbrewing
Facebook: www.facebook.com/hessbrewing

2010 Production: 37 BBL
2011 Production: 183 BBL

Brewery Hours:

W-TH 2 to 7 pm, Friday 2 to 8 pm, Saturday 1pm to 5pm.

About the Brewery:

Undoubtedly if you were to type in "nanobrewery" into your favorite search engine you will be led to the Hess Brewing Blog which has a very nice listing of the country's operating and in planning nanobreweries. It is THE place to go on the internet to find out where your local nano is located.

If I had to describe the brewery in four words or less I would say "busting at the seams" is pretty good. They cranked out an eye-popping 183 BBL's in 2011 on essentially a 3 BBL system. "As soon as a fermenter is emptied and cleaned it is being filled with another batch of beer, there is no down time at the brewery," says owner and brewer Mike Hess.

If you want the beer you will more than likely have to visit the brewery, "We sell about 98% of our beer on site". But you won't have to worry about them not having your favorite brew...by the time you read this they may have already moved into their new facility (don't worry, they are still keeping the old one) that will have a 17,000 BBL capacity! "People in San Diego love beer and they really are loving our

beer." Says Mike. "I always wanted a large brewery but this happened quicker than even I expected."

On a quarterly basis they have brewed more beer than they have the previous quarter for 8 consecutive quarters when I talked to Mike, he also mentioned he doesn't expect that trend to change for some time.

Hess does growlers and pints at the brewery with 7-8 beers on tap at all times. You won't see Hess in bottles though, "We keg 100% of our beer…right now." (Secret is out though, there is a picture of their new canning line being delivered on their Facebook page!)

His advice to future nano-brewers is "Good beer doesn't guarantee success. Remember, a brewery is a business, not just a place where beer is made. Think about how you are going to run the business of beer before you start."

Beers:

"We don't make any 'need-to' beers. We don't make an amber or a generic pale ale," says Mike about their beer lineup. "There is too much competition is San Diego for that type of stuff."

He does say that the #1 seller is probably *Grazias*. It is a Vienna Cream Ale that is smooth and sweet. "It ferments quickly so we can keep it on tap at all times, which is key."

Their best reviewed beer online is *Ex Umbris*, an Imperial Stout brewed with Rye for a nice spiciness. Many say the bitterness is perfect and goes down incredibly smooth for a 9.8% ABV beer.

This will be a sad loss to the nano-brewery community when they expand but they have earned it…cheers!

Idle Hands Craft Ales

Address: 3 Charlton Street, Bld 3, Unit 4
                Everett, MA
Website: www.idlehandscraftales.com
Twitter: @idlehandsbeer
Facebook: www.facebook.com/idlehandscraftales

2010 Production: N/A
2011 Production: 27 BBL

Brewery Hours: Saturdays Noon to 4pm

<u>About the Brewery:</u>

Chris and Grace Tkach are the owners at this 1.5 BBL nano. I spoke
with Grace and she gave me the low down on Idle Hands, "Chris has
been brewing since he was 21 and at some point when his current 'day
job' was getting old, he decided to put his MBA to better use and start a
brewery. Getting married helped with that as well - knowing that
someone else was there to bear some of the risk."

All this time Chris was ripping through homebrew competitions and
winning several of them…

"More specifically, we had been discussing our future once we got
married and threw around a lot of business ideas - we both had the
entrepreneur bug and got our MBA's thinking we'd someday own our
own businesses. Chris was always reading about breweries and started
reading more and more about the idea of a nanobrewery."

After a trip to a nanobrewery they said "we can do this", and went
forward with their own plans. "After seeing a real nanobrewery in the
works and learning it had only taken him about 9 months to cover the
cost of this 'hobby', we agreed it would be a good, relatively lower risk

place to start. At the very least, it could be a self-funding hobby - at best, we could grow it into a sustaining business."

You can get their beers at local restaurants and pubs but they also do growlers on site with 6 beers available for sampling. They also bottle some of their beer.

Don't expect them to be "nano" for too long though… "We started off as a nanobrewery intentionally to make sure we could make the concept work. Now that we've had success for 6+ months, we're looking into expanding our capacity in the near future. We moved into our space knowing we'd want to grow so we'll be spending the next few months figuring the logistics out and of course looking for financing. This is all of course, while we continue to operate at the scale we're at."

Beers:

You won't find off-the-wall beers at Idle Hands…"We see ourselves as more of a purist brewery so experimenting is more along the lines of trying new styles or bending existing ones. You won't find us throwing exotic/non-traditional ingredients in our beers. That's not what we are about. However, we do use spices in some of our beers but always at a level that complements the flavors in the beer versus beating you over the head with them. That being said, we do have a barrel program whereby we have several different sours and other barrel-aged beers working their magic in the barrel. None of them have been released yet."

Their "flagship" is the *Pandora*, a Belgian Pale Ale made with Magnum, Goldings, Aurora, & Cascade Hops. "It's medium bodied beer that marries the light fruit and spice characteristics of the Idle Hands house yeast with the hoppiness of an APA."

70

Ishii Brewing Company

Address: #102 Northwest Plaza
                 458 South Marine Corps Drive
                 Tamuning, Guam 96931
Website: www.Ishiibrew.com
Twitter: N/A
Facebook: N/A

2010 Production: 13 BBL
2011 Production: 77 BBL

Brewery Hours: N/A

About the Brewery:

Hey, if Guam gets electoral votes in Presidential Primaries I am counting their brewery as US breweries…and technically they fall under the federal governments guidelines so they are a US brewery.

Anyway there is a good chance that you have tried a beer from the owner Toshi Ishii even though he doesn't distribute in the continental United States.

He and his brewery participated in the *Baird / Ishii / Stone Japanese Green Tea IPA* which was made to support the relief effort in Japan after the tsunami. Toshi told me that, "This is the first collaboration beer brewed as a fundraiser."

"I worked under the greatest mentor Steve Wagner (current Stone Brewing Co. President), while at Stone." Says Toshi and they collaborated on this truly unique brew.

He is also pumping out some very cool beers on his ½ BBL (15.5 gallon) Sabco® Brew Magic in Guam. Ishii Brewing is Guam's first and only brewery.

71

None of the beer is filtered or pasteurized and is always served fresh throughout Guam. You can find it in several bars and restaurants as well as in growlers at the brewery.

Beers:

"There are no adjuncts in our beer, only the best ingredients go into the beer." Says Toshi about his brews.

He currently offers two *MINOGAF* brand beers. Toshi tells me that the word, "means pleasure, joy, happiness and chee in local language."

The Pale Ale is made with Warrior and Ahtnum hops that gives off a nice citrusy floral flavor.

The second offering from the brewery is an IPA made with a nice mesh of Magnum, Centennial, Amarillo, and dry-hopped with Columbus hops.

He is planning on doing some other island style beers. "Now I'm planning to brew with some wild yeasts and any spices which are very famous and used for a local alcohol on Guam. It should be crazy style like experimental sour island-style ale."

Keg and Barrel / Southern Prohibition Brewery

Address: 1315 Hardy Street
                Hattiesburg MS, 39401
Website: www.kegandbarrel.com
Twitter: @SoProBrewCo
Facebook: Yes

2010 Production: 40 BBL
2011 Production: 80 BBL

Brewery Hours: M-W 3pm – 1am, T-SA 3pm to 2am, Su 3pm to 11pm

About the Brewery:

John Neal is the owner of the 1 BBL brewery that is located inside on the Top 100 bars in the country as per *Draft Magazines* 2010 and 2011 rankings. John believes the ranking comes in part from the beer. "We specialize in creating fun, unique, and delicious craft beers."

They are always changing up what is on tap at the brewery. "Beer is constantly being filled and emptied out of the fermenters due to the demand from our thirsty patrons. We also take advantage of ales we place in firkins and oak barrels."

They will also benefit from a new law that allows for beer to be manufactured at an ABW up to 8% (it previously was only 5% ABW).

All the Southern Prohibition beer is sold on site in pints, they do not distribute. There are always at least two Southern Prohibition beers on tap at the Keg and Barrel at all times but they hope to increase that soon. "As far as future plans for the brewery you'll just have to keep your ear to the ground but we diligently working on starting a 20BBL brew house in downtown Hattiesburg and using the nano as our experimental system." Says John about possible expansion.

Beers:

Sure, you'll find some regular pale ales in their lineup but when you have a plethora of other breweries beer on tap there you can really experiment.

"Our most experimental beers are the watermelon wheat ale with 3 watermelons added to the fermenter and a rye saison with lavender and basil."

They've also done a chili amber ale and a few other off the wall types of beers, "Although all patrons' palates are different, for the most part we cannot produce beer fast enough and everything is well received."

The owner tells me his personal favorites are a rye pale ale called "*Pow... Rye in the Kisser*" and their IPA with Apollo hops called "*Apollo Creed IPA*"

They also offer some cool flights of beers as you can see by their facebook.com picture update.

Lantern Brewing

Address: 7410 Greenwood Ave N
                Seattle, WA
Website: www.lanternbrewing.com
Twitter: @lanternbrewing
Facebook: www.facebook.com/lanternbrewing

2010 Production: N/A
2011 Production: 13 BBL

Brewery Hours: N/A

About the Brewery:

What I can say about the brewery…it is a nano, after that…not much. Reviews and reviewers are scarce, and I did send a letter as a last resort (you know the thing you put a stamp on and actually WRITE OUT), and couldn't connect with them.

Beers:

Triple Abbey-Style Golden Ale is their best reviewed beer online and the reviews that are out there comment on the nice malty taste it has as opposed to just an alcohol burn.

Listermann Brewing Supply / Triple Digit Brewing

Address: 1621 Dana Ave
                   Cincinnati OH
Website: www.listermann.com
Twitter: @Listermann
Facebook: Yes

2010 Production: N/A
2011 Production: N/A

Brewery Hours: M-SAT 10am – 6pm

About the Brewery:

Homebrewers are always dreaming of opening a nanobrewery. Pickin
out supplies at the local homebrew shop is where you can learn some
tricks of the trade from other homebrewers...or in this case an actual
brewer.

Triple Digit Brewing is inside the Listermann Brewing Supply store in
Cincinnati Ohio.

While the primary business is still the brew shop, owner Dan
Listermann figured an on-site brewery would be the perfect fit to brin
in more customers and could be used as a tool to teach people how to
brew.

Dan says "We would have liked a bigger brewhouse, but we didn't
have the space we wanted so we have a 2 BBL brewery." They serve
beer by the pint, in the growler, and also the occasional bottle release.

Not all the beer is served on site though, "We do deliver to the
occasional local tavern."

Dan is planning to open a larger brewery somewhere down the line to serve more of the beer. "I want to lose the 'nano' and become a brewery."

Demand is high for the beer and they are constantly brewing. If you want to learn how to brew beer why not do it at an actual brewery that sells all the supplies you'll ever need?

Dan says he only had one disaster at the brewery so far, "I needed a valve and I took one of a full mash tun." I am sure the cleanup from that one was nothing but good times...

Beers:

One of the more popular releases at the brewery was the *Cincinnatus 2011 Bourbon Barrel Aged Stout.* They were released in bottles and #'d out of 2,324 total bottles.

This is a very popular beer among beer reviewers that point out its wonderful Whiskey like taste.

Other brewery favorites are the Double Black IPA, and the Aftermath – A Scottish Style Ale that is frequently on tap at the brewery.

Millbock Brewing Company

Address:
Website: www.millbock.com
Twitter: @Millbock
Facebook: www.facebook.com/millbock

2010 Production: N/A
2011 Production: 10 BBL

Brewery Hours: None

About the Brewery:

I would have loved to have talked to this new nano in PA but couldn't get in contact with the brewers. Luckily I have a buddy in Harrisburg from my old days in politics so he was able to give me some info on a few of their beers.

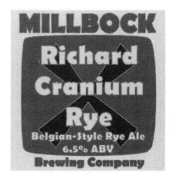

Gotta love these guys, they built their own brewery by hand and put together some equipment so they could start brewing. Unfortunately they don't have any on site sales but they can be found in and around Harrisburg. They bottle and keg their beer.

Beers:

My friend (who asked to remain anonyms, I guess he doesn't want to admit friendship), said he was a big fan of the *Richard Cranium Rye*, a Belgian Styled Rye Ale. "It's got a nice thick head from the pour and a wonderful banana/clove aroma. The rye gives it a hint of spice which absolutely love; I will get this one again."

His next beer was the Millbock White, "Another nice pouring beer, great look. I am also a fan of this one, nice yeasty finish to a light bodied beer."

Mo's Place Grill and Brewpub

Address: 1908 Elm Street
              Beaver, KN 67525
Website: www.mosbrewpub.com
Twitter: n/a
Facebook: n/a

2010 Production: 46 BBL
2011 Production: 37 BBL

Brewery Hours: W-SA 10:30am to 9pm

About the Brewery:

Hank from *Hank is Wiser Brewing* told me about Mo's Place. "He is literally in the middle of nowhere, and in Kansas that is really out there." Beaver, Kansas is a "suburb" of Claflin City (Population 705), so there aren't many people there, but if they are, they are drinking at Mo's.

Mo is running a local bar and brewing up his own ales. Whether you want to shoot pool, play some arcade games, or sit at the bar and B.S. with buddies, all is welcome at Mo's.

He runs a ½ BBL system but has plenty of other breweries beers on tap and in bottles. All of Mo's beer is sold on site. Mo has a full menu of food with down home cooking like burgers, gizzards, livers, okra, and ribeye steak.

Beers:

The Harvest Moon wheat packs in a grain bill of 35% wheat malt (which is a lot), and has all German hops for a crisp finish. *The Elm Street Porter has* 5 different malts and Perle and Cascade Hops. There aren't any crazy one-off beers at Mo's just solid beer served up daily.

Mr. Grumpy Pants Brewing Company / Ourayle House Brewery

Address: 215 7th Ave
                    Ouray, CO 81427
Website: www.ouraylehouse.com
Twitter: N/A
Facebook: N/A

2010 Production: 75 BBL
2011 Production: 280 BBL

Brewery Hours: They have them.

About the Brewery:

I really tried to hunt down the owner for this one, (even sent a letter), but couldn't get in contact with them.

Fortunately, I found Chris Allen (@domingo_x) of Colorado who had actually been to the brewery. Chris told me this about the place, *"I'd absolutely go back. The owner/brewer was a wacky guy that really loved what he did. The place looked like a mix of an old tool shed and a cabin in the wilderness. The vibe of the brewery was off the charts weird, which is the kind of places I tend to enjoy. Ourayle brewing seems like a pretty serious operation, so hopefully "Mr. Grumpy Pants" has his own following."*

The only thing I could confirm is they have a 1 or maybe now a 2 BBL system at the brewery.

Beers:

I'd like to include info on at least 1 beer but I honestly couldn't find any.

Naked City Brewing

Address: 8564 Greenwood Ave N
               Seattle WA, 98103
Website: www.nakedcitybrewing.com
Twitter: @NakedCityBeer
Facebook: Yes

2010 Production: 169 BBL
2011 Production: 235 BBL

Brewery Hours: M-T 3pm to Midnight, W-TH 12 to 11pm, F-SA 12 to Midnight, Sunday 12 to 10pm.

About the Brewery:

Don Webb and Donald Averill co-own the Seattle based brewery. They are a "big" nanobrewery with a 4 BBL brewing system and it is getting a workout.

They are like most nanobrewers, "We have a passion for brewing great craft beer and we wanted to share that passion." Says their General Manager Brian Miller.

They serve their beers on tap at their bar, and I have to imagine they have something for everyone available at the bar. "We have a 160-person brewpub with a full kitchen, 24-rotating taps including about 6 house beers, 4 cider taps, 2 wine taps, and a root beer tap. We also have a dining movie theatre called the Screening Room."

They are selling their beer more and more each month and will be making way for more capacity in 2012. "We're awaiting the arrival of 4 new 10BBL fermenters and 2 16BBL Bright Tanks here in the next few weeks. We're keeping the same 4BBL Brew Kettle and Mash Tun."

They also have the coolest website in the nanobrewery business hands-down. It is a must visit. Very cool film noire look and feel.

Beers:

Brian gave me the rundown on three of their better selling beers. "*Hoptrocity* – 9.5% ABV, 95 IBU, Imperial Rye IPA. 18% rye malt lends a spiciness that accentuates the intense Centennial, Zythos and Amarillo hop profile while additional malts provide the perfect balance of sweetness.

Fleur D' Elise - 5.6% ABV, Saison. Unfiltered Farmhouse Ale brewed with Orris Root, Grains of Paradise and primed with Orange Blossom Honey.

Betsy's Mountain – 6% ABV, 28 IBU, Brown. Brewed in honor of General Manager Bryan's mom--also the woman who gave owner Donald his first beer--Betsy's Mountain holds a summer sunset from the north face of Mt. Rainier in its clear amber light. With a smoky nose and a complex finish, Betsy's Mountain is the complete package. Much like the woman herself."

The most sought after beer at the brewery is one they don't even brew all time. "It's the Hoptrocity. The Rye IPA with a dedicated following in Seattle. We only brew it a few times a year and it always draws a crowd."

When I asked if they were into experimenting Brian said, "We're always experimenting! Head Brewer Don loves to innovate with unique styles and combinations. *NC-17*, our *Honey Dew Malt Liquor* was a hit at the Portland Fruit Beer Festival. Recently, our *Dude in Every Port*—a Kahlua-infused Imperial Cream Stout aged in a Port Wine Barrel—had a good showing at Seattle's Cask Beer Festival."

Natian Brewery

Address: 1321 NE Couch St
                  Portland, OR 97232
Website: www.natianbrewing.com
Twitter: @NatianBrewery
Facebook: www.facebook.com/natianbrewing

2010 Production: N/A
2011 Production: 100 BBL

Brewery Hours: None

About the Brewery:

They are brewing 100 BBL's of beer...one barrel at a time..."We are a 1 BBL brewery and we do it for the love of the beer." Says owner/brewer Ian McGuinness.

He and fellow brewer Natalia Laird are brewing frequently and doing something incredibly unique for any craft brewer, let alone a nanobrewery... "We are first microbrewery in Portland Oregon to offer beer in aluminum cans." You "can" find limited amount of their beer in 16 oz. cans throughout Portland.

They also offer the beer to bars on tap but do not have on site sales.

While they enjoy the freedom of the small system they are in the works of expanding to a 10 BBL system in 2013.

Beers:

They brew just about everything at the brewery. They have 3 flagship beers and tons of seasonals. Some of their more popular beers are the: *LumberJane Stout*, a black ale with some smoke and a heavy bite. The *Big Block IPA*, and the *Undun Blonde Ale*.

Night Shift Brewing

Address: 3 Charleston Street
                 Everett, MA 02149
Website: www.nightshiftbrewing.com
Twitter: @nightshiftbeer
Facebook: www.facebook.com/nightshiftbeer

2010 Production: N/A
2011 Production: N/A

Brewery Hours: T-TH 5pm to 9pm, Sat noon to 5pm

About the Brewery:

Three friends who were avid homebrewers decided to take their passion to the next level in the winter of 2012. "We didn't have formal training so we figured we better start small so we can get a solid grasp on what we are doing before we go larger," says Michael Oxton a Co-Founder of Night Shift.

"We want to focus of innovative and unorthodox beers. We take a chef like mentality to beer trying to pair unique flavors and ingredient with traditional beer ingredients."

The brewery is also set up to take on visitors. "We wanted the brewery to be accessible. You can see the brewing process from start to finish the brewery and really learn how we make it." They also have 2 oz. sample pours and growlers/bottles available for sale on site along with some merchandise.

You can also find their beer in bars and restaurants throughout the region on draft and in 750 ml champagne bottles. Michael told me they bottle a little over half of the beer they make.

They have plans to expand to a larger brewing system down the road, "…but we really don't have a timetable yet, we are just getting our feet wet for now." Says Michael.

Beers:

"Memorable beer is what we are trying to make." And what is more memorable than a Habanero Rye beer? I can think of nothing. "This will be released down the road but we have tested at the brewery and people love it." It doesn't have extreme heat, just a nice warming taste.

They started selling a large amount of the *Bee Tea* which is a wheat ale with honey and green tea but things changed in the summer. "We found there is a huge market for *Somer Weiss*. "It's a Berliner-Weiss style beer with lemongrass, ginger, and a hint of sourness. We weren't sure if people would accept it but we can't brew enough of it right now."

They also make a *Taza Stout* made with chicory.

In the future they plan on making more and more exotic beers and adding a larger barrel aging program. "We'd love to add a ton of barrels in here towards the end of the year and start making some more memorable beer."

NW Peaks Brewery

Address: 4912 17th Ave NW
                      Seattle WA
Website: www.nwpeaksbrewery.com
Twitter: @NWPeaksBrewery
Facebook: www.facebook.com/NWPeaksBrewery

2010 Production: 2 BBL
2011 Production: 40 BBL

Brewery Hours: Varying, check site for latest update

About the Brewery:

Kevin Klein is the founder and head brewmaster at this 1 BBL brewery. He talked a little about why he opened a nano. "Love for beer, love for variation in beer, friends pushing me to be able to sell my beer because it was as good as most commercial beers, and mostly the desire to get a foot into the industry to see if it was "for me" without going full steam ahead into a Microbrewery."

"Changes may be coming at the brewery, as I have gotten the foot in the door and want to grow the nano to micro level. So we're looking some market evaluation to see which direction we'll move - bottles, kegs, styles, wholesale, retail, tap room/bar, etc."

One of the most successful ventures Kevin has done is his "Mountain Beers" program. "It's really setup for locals." You get a growler of whatever the new beer is each month before anyone else can get their hands on it. You just come in, exchange your empty for a full one and you're on your way.

Most of the beer is distributed out of the brewery in growlers (or the occasional bottle), but they also serve their beer in and around Seattle in a handful of local bars.

Beers:

Instead of having some flagship beers Kevin likes to change it up. They have 2 new beers each month. "It allows us to brew more styles of beer."

One of those beers Kevin told me about was his biggest risk, "*Agassiz Acai* hands down." I have had Acai (similar to the blueberry) beers before but never one like this…

"We brewed Agassiz with more than 60 percent rice. However we didn't stop there. We added cooked rice to the fermenter…yes, the fermenter…to try to leach a bunch of the starches and rice character from the rice. We all know that light beers made with rice have no rice character and virtually no character at all). We then used sake yeast to ferment the beer. After fermenting we threw a kink into the "sake beer" idea and added Acai puree to get a nice fruit balance on top of the starchy rice backbone." That is insane and I am pissed I live nowhere near Seattle.

The other beer I was curious about was the *Spickard Spiced Ale*. "While many breweries are doing pumpkin spice beers in October, we decided to wait until November. And instead of using Halloween spices (pumpkin), we went towards Thanksgiving spices/ingredients. We started with a base that includes more than 25% maize giving the beer a thicker, sweeter flavor. We then added some spruce, rosemary, and thyme that give the beer a flavor reminiscent of thanksgiving stuffing."

On The Tracks Brewery

Address: 5674 El Camino Real
               Carlsbad, CA 92008
Website: www.ottbrew.com
Twitter: N/A
Facebook: Yes

2010 Production: N/A
2011 Production: 30 BBL

Brewery Hours: TH 4:30 to 7:30, F 4 to 9:30, SA 1 to 9, SU 1 to 4

About the Brewery:

A self-described Scottish/English style brewery that focuses on the "Darker Side of Beer". I couldn't connect with the owners or brewers but they give a great description of why they went into their business and about their passion for beer on their website.

Beers:

There was not 1 beer review online I could find of this place but they are doing some unique ales including the *Baltic Pepper Porter* which has Pepper Corns and Jalapeño.

Probably the most unique for the *Peary Pale Ale* which is made with local Julian Peaches and is a Cider/Pale Ale Hybrid.

Oak Hills Brewing Company

Address: 12221 Poplar Street
                Hespiria CA
Website: www.oakhillsbrewing.com
Twitter: @oakhillsbrewing
Facebook: www.facebook.com/oakhillsbrewing

2010 Production: N/A
2011 Production: N/A

Brewery Hours: None yet

<u>About the Brewery:</u>

When I talked to Joy Connolly she was happy to tell me they have ordered a 7 BBL brewery and will hopefully be up and running in late 2012 with their larger brewery but were happy they started small, "We wanted to start a brewing company, and started at the "Nano" size to keep costs down and do a "Proof of Concept" i.e., to make sure that there's a market for us."…And there was.

They plan to serve most if not all the beer from the future tasting room. "Initially, all our sales will be though our tasting room. Then we will distribute kegs to local bars and restaurants as we grow. Bottling and canning will happen down the road."

She does offer some of the best advice you'll ever hear to a future nanobrewery, "Double everything in your plans: timeline, costs, etc."

<u>Beers:</u>

They don't have a flagship beer yet, but are close. "Not yet, but we did a test batch of a Belgian Tripel that was very well received. Being in the desert, we'll focus mainly on lighter beers (Pale ales, Kolsch, etc.). Not to say that we won't have big, dark, and/or heavy beers, just that the environment lends to lighter beers."

Puyallup River Brewing

Address: South Hill, Puyallup, WA 98375
Website: www.puyallu,priverbrewing.com
Twitter: @puyallupbrew
Facebook: www.facebook.com/puyallupriverbrewing

2010 Production: N/A
2011 Production: N/A

Brewery Hours: None

About the Brewery:

This is one of the freshest nanobreweries in the US and makes Puyallup the nanobrewery capital with two (*DUO Brewing*) in the same town.

Eric got it started in the winter of 2012 and has been pumping out as much beer as his 1 BBL system could handle. "I am selling literally every drop of beer I produce as soon as it is ready." Says Eric.

While the system may be small he has two 3 BBL fermenters and thre 1 BBL fermenters.

"I use the space as best as I can and I think I could squeeze a 3 BBL brewhouse in the brewery space." That space is a 500 square foot brew space built by Eric on his home property. "It's the largest the town would allow so I made it as big as I could."

Currently there are no on site sales, but you can find the beer throughout the area around him. "I hand bottle about 80% of the bee I make and the rest goes into kegs." That's a crazy amount to bottle and kudos to Eric for taking the time to do it.

He points out that he is trying to stick out in the market by being a little different. "I couldn't come out with a hoppy IPA and expect to compete. I like doing things that are unique but not over the top…I really want to make sure you get a really clean tasting beer."

Beers:

In the short time Eric has been up and running he has found that his saison is the most popular pick. "It's my favorite style and locals are really starting to get into it. There aren't many in the Washington market so I enjoy it when people 'discover' the style"

Eric plans on doing several variations on the Saison as he moves forward. "It's been so well received I need to do more of it."

His *Frying Pan Cascadian Red Ale* is another local favorite. It has copious amounts of Magnum, Amarillo Gold, and Centennial Hops. It comes in at 7% ABV and is the second best seller so far.

"I'm trying to experiment with beers that haven't been too popular in the Northwest; most beers are hop forward so I am trying to do something different. I like more balanced malty beers so that's what I am trying to put out there."

Red Ear Brewing

Address: 208 Pike Street
             Covington, KY 41011
Website: www.redearbrewing.com
Twitter: @RedEarBrew
Facebook: Yes

2010 Production: 20 BBL
2011 Production: 25 BBL

Brewery Hours: Saturdays (Variable)

About the Brewery:

Mike DeDomenico and Matt Wehmeyer own Red Ear and started pretty humble. "We brewed beer in small 5 gallon batches and slowly gained confidence over time. As confidence grew in our abilities we took one additional step at a time and began to believe we could make "this" happen." Says Mike.

"This" was new Sabco ½ BBL brewing system, they are now doing 2 BBL batches.

Mike told me they do growlers and also have their beer at bars throughout the area.

They are also big into the local community. "We are unique because we are two guys that live and love beer and will only put out product that we would drink. We use local products where we can and support our community in every way, shape or form. Try our beer because it is local and fresh."

When I asked them what their most popular beer was they were torn, "*Cattail Pale Ale* or our *M.A.D. Alex Chocolate Oatmeal Stout.*"

The Cattail is in honor of our Wildcat, Bearcat and Bengal cat heritage. This classic American Pale Ale has caramel like features with a rich malty start and just the right amount of hop bitterness at the "tail" end.

The stout is a traditional Irish Stout brewed with plenty of oats and just the right amount of roasted chocolate malts. It pours deep black with a rich head and finishes with a gentle bitterness.

Rumspringa Brewing

Address: 3174 Old Philadelphia Pike
                Bird-In-Hand PA, 17505
Website: www.lancaster-gallery.com
Twitter: N/A
Facebook: Yes

2010 Production: N/A
2011 Production: 15 BBL

Brewery Hours: M-Sa 10am to 6pm and Sunday 11am to 6pm.

About the Brewery:

Local cheese, wine and beer are what you can expect when you head out to the Rumspinga Brewery located in the heart of Amish country in Pennsylvania. The brewery is on the 2nd floor of what was already a successful wine shop. "The wine part was successful so we decided to add a brewery to the 2nd floor." Says head brewer Mike Osborne.

The word "Rumspringa" is actually German and a nice description of the word is found on the company website. "A popularized view of "rumspringa" reflects on the term used to describe a temporary period when young members of Amish communities start dating and going places on their own, exploring activities in the 'outside world'. "

You can enjoy the beer (or the wine) right on site in The Barn Café. They have a menu that matches very well with the beers and wines offered. They serve all their beer on site in pints and growlers but even bottle some of it.

Mike says it is a great place to visit along your travels. "We located in a very unique location in the heart of Lancaster County Amish Country. It's located between Bird-in-Hand and Intercourse, PA. A nice place to stop, get some beer samples, have a pint, and try some local cheeses while you tour Amish Country."

If you are into the country feel there is nothing more country then hanging out in a bar that is in a barn.

Beers:

If you are in Amish country you need a great German beer. Rumspringa's answer is the Harvest Gold. A Kolsch made with German Tettnanger hops with has a nice soft finish.

While they don't have too many off the wall beers they do offer a Chocolate Blackberry Stout which is picking up fans at the brewery.

Their most popular beer is definitely The Red Caboose Amber. "It's our best seller," says Mike, "it's a medium-bodied Amber Ale, brewed with all English ingredients. English caramel malts add to the color and flavor."

They are looking to add more seasonals to the lineup as they go forward.

Soos Creek Brewing

Address: Covington WA, 98042
Website: www.sooscreekbrewingco.com
Twitter: @Soosbrew
Facebook: www.facebook.com/soos.creek.brewing.co

2010 Production: N/A
2011 Production: 16 BBL

Brewery Hours: None

About the Brewery:

Soos Creek is a 1 BBL nano trying to get a foothold in the Washington craft beer market.

They currently do not serve beer at the brewery in growlers, but they do sell their kegs for home use and you can pick those up at the brewery. Right now they are distributing their kegs throughout the Covington area.

Beers:

Soos Creek focuses on solid balanced beers. They currently offer four beers: An Irish Red, A Dark Cascadian, an ESB and a Bohemian Pilsner.

Squam Brewing Company

Address: 118 Perch Pond Road
                 Holderness, NH 03245
Website: www.squambrewing.com
Twitter: @squambrewing
Facebook: Yes

2010 Production: 10 BBL
2011 Production: 30 BBL

Brewery Hours: None

About the Brewery:

This is one of the rare nano's that exclusively bottle their beer. "No kegs, just bottles," says owner John Glidden.

He started his brewery because he was getting sick of "the daily grind"

Squam makes all of their beers on a 1.5 BBL system that is backed up by seven 42 gallons fermenters. He makes 9 beers annually so this allows him to change it up frequently.

He also has a nice business of personalized beers. "The possibilities ar endless, I get requests for all types of beers." You'll walk away with 1! cases of your very own beer bottled at a brewery.

He doesn't serve on site and distributes the bottles throughout the are in anywhere in between 12-15 different spots from bars to supermarkets.

John is looking to expand but is not sure if and when that is going to happen, "I'd like a 7 Barrel System but not sure when that will happen."

Beers:

The Golden IPA is Squams best reviewed beer on the web. Most reviewers classify it as fruity and citrusy with a nice finish.

The highest ABV beer in the lineup is *The Camp*, a Barley Wine with a malty bread like taste and a nice fruity apple like finish. You'll notice the beautiful label. All the labels are watercolor pictures done by a local artist. Art in the bottle, art on the bottle.

Three Barrel Brewery

Address: 586 Columbia Street
                  Del Norte, CO
Website: www.threebarrelbrew.com
Twitter: @brickermeister
Facebook: Yes

2010 Production: 131 BBL
2011 Production: 84 BBL

Brewery Hours: Coming Soon

<u>About the Brewery:</u>

I'll give you one guess as to the size of the brewery…3 Barrels is correct. If you are reading this they may have already reconstructed their tasting room and have a very nice brewery tasting room for you to sample their beers in.

They have some very nice 4 BBL fermenters on site that allow them t crank out a lot of beer.

Their new tasting room will be a large area that serves all of the Thre Barrel Brews on tap. Currently they serve other bars but that may change if demand exceeds expectations at the brewery.

Another rarity for nano's they have some very professional copper equipment that looks beautiful. Many nano's (Like mine) look more like a backyard meth lab than a brewery. If you are into brewing it i worth the trip to check out.

<u>Beers:</u>

Unfortunately their website doesn't do more than list their beers witl no description and there are no reviews online ☹

Twisted Vine Brewery

Address: 3021 St Charles Road
              Saint Charles, IA 50240
Website: www.twistedvinebrewery.com
Twitter:
Facebook: www.facebook.com/twistedvine

2010 Production: N/A
2011 Production: 10 BBL

Brewery Hours: Varying

About the Brewery:

The "Unpretentious" brewery is located inside the Madison County Winery in Iowa. Steve Breman, Steve Becker, and Brian Sabus took their homebrewing hobby to the next level and opened up their 1 BBL brewery in the heart of Iowa wine country.

Most of their beer is served on site, but you will find their ales in local bars in the area.

The three owners all work other jobs but wanted another part time job to spread their love of beer with the rest of the region.

Beers:

They have a pretty cool idea, do 8 regular all season beers then sprinkle in the seasonals.

These are their 8 go-to beers: Blonde, Amber, Wheat, American Pale, Black IPA, Porter, Red, and a Scottish Ale.

In the summer they also make a Saison.

Valholl Brewing Company

Address: 20186 Front Steet NE, Suite B
              Poulsbo, WA 98370
Website: www.vahollbrewing.com
Twitter: @valhollbrew
Facebook: www.facebook.com/valhollbrewing

2011 Production: 24 BBL

Brewery Hours: Thursday – Sat 4pm to 9pm Sunday noon to 6pm

About the Brewery:

This Viking inspired brewery is owned by Jeff Holcomb, Jordan Rodgers, Aaron Kallio, and Bill Ready. They operate a ½ BBL Sabco machine and another 3.5 BBL Ager tank.

"Jordan and I were brewers at the now closed Heads Up Brewing Company in Washington. When it closed its doors we knew we had to get our own place open. The brewing bug had been planted and I knew this was to be my new career. We scrapped our money together and opened our doors in 201 with a 15000 dollar budget. That took off and we now own a building and are expanding very rapidly." That comes from Jeff.

They have a full tasting room that serves both pints and growlers. While they are enjoying their current success they are looking toward the future. "We want to expand from 90 bbl per year to 1400 bbl per year with 3 year plan to move into a 30 bbl production brewery." When Jeff was asked about their future plans.

He also had the best (Or worst depending on how you look at it), disaster story about working in a brewery. "I was brewing the Firkin Hammer and while moving a glass carboy it exploded and sliced my leg to the bone. I tied it off then walked my friend through finishing the beer before I let them take me to the hospital. A nice scar helps me remember."

While most of their beer is served on site, they do make rounds to a few of the local taverns by dropping off some kegs here and there.

If you are looking for variety they currently have 46 recipes for beers and are always looking to expand upon that.

<u>Beers:</u>

If you want something different, you have come to the right place: session beers, fruit beers, high ABV, rhubarb...nothing is off limits.

Probably their most off the wall beer is *Hildisvini* (Battle Boar) "it was collaboration with Dave Lambert of Slippery Pig Brewing. A weird Belgian beer brewed with caramelized summer squash, rhubarb, raisins, brown sugar, finished with trappist yeast. We took third place at Strange Brewfest with it."

Their best sellers at the bar are a trio of beers. "Stouty Stouteson, Valkyrie Red and Firkin Hammer. Because they take normal styles and twist them to make them unique in some way."

Let's look deeper into the Stouty Stouteson to see just what that "twist" is all about...They put Sweet Potatoes in the mash and add cinnamon, raisins, and brown sugar to the mix. Did I mention it has a 13% ABV?

They also offer a host of other beers that are sure to test your palate and frequently update their webpage with what they are offering.

Wit's End Brewing Company ™

Address: 2505 W 2nd Ave, Unit #13
                      Denver CO, 80219
Website: www.witsendbrewing.com
Twitter: @WitsEndBrewing
Facebook: www.facebook.com/witsendbrewing

2010 Production: N/A
2011 Production: 26 BBL

Brewery Hours: TH 4pm to 8pm, F-SA 2pm to 8pm, SU noon to 5pm

About the Brewery:

Scott Witsoe is the owner/brewer at Wit's End Brewing Company and he is doing it all on a 1 Barrel system that is brewing up some great beer that locals are falling in love with.

The brewery has a tasting room attached were you can buy a pint or fill up a 40 ounce metal "growler".

I must say I am greatly impressed by these, much more useful than the glass ones; I may have to do some shopping myself!

The taproom has a very cool unpretentious setup, focusing on the beer. "This is my favorite place to grab a pint in Denver and that is saying alot because there are so many places to drink here," one anonyms local told me.

"Scott is a great guy who knows his beer and makes some damn good stuff."

Scott self distributes and along with his pub sales he has the beer in local bars and restaurants.

They also have a very nice online store where you can land some cool brewery "Schwag".

Beers:

It's all about the beer…Scott has 4 "Core" beers that are almost always available but there are experimental ones. The core ones cover all bases, *Jean Claude Van-Blonde, Super FL i.p.a, Green Man Ale, and Kitchen Sink Porter.*

His coolest experimental ale may be the *Ugly Sweater.* It is an English Brown with roasted pumpkin seeds and palm sugar.

He also did the *Wilford,* a Belgian Oatmeal IPA…that sounds awesome.

If you take a look online, the reviews are solid and he seems to be picking up new customers daily so he may not be a nano for too long!

Damn, this book is already done?

Craft beer should be fun and interesting. The last thing I want you to do is take 4 months to read a book about beer. It shouldn't be consuming that much of your time (or maybe you're just a really slow reader).

I really wanted you to read this in a weekend, get amped up about all these new places you read about and start planning your next road trip. These places are always changing up their beer lineups but they can't unless you go there and drink it!

Last Call

Thanks again for buying the book!

I'd like this to be a complete book, so if you find there isn't a brewery in here and it should be please email me with whatever info you have to Dan@beaverbrewingcompany.com

I'd also encourage you to seek out these places. They are brewing up some of the best beer in the business and if you don't go there and try their beer don't be the one complaining when your next stop at the bar has 5 boring macro brewed beers on tap with no variety.

It's also great for you to request these beers at your local tavern. Tap space is hard to find in plenty of towns and it is a big help when fans request it out at the brewery.

When you do stop in these places let them know how you found out about them. It's great to hear how people found out about my brewery, it lets me know what I am doing is working and I know other brewers really appreciate it too.

Whatever you do, drink LOCAL beer. It doesn't have to be from a nano-brewery, but if you see some local on tap at the very least give it a try.

The money you spend on that pint will go towards keeping people in your community employed and your hometown will stay vibrant.

Again, thanks for buying the book, I'd really like you to visit the Beaver Brewing Company Facebook, twitter, and homepage if you have a chance and if you are ever in the Beaver Falls metro area I'd love you to stop in a share a beer!

Made in the USA
San Bernardino, CA
04 May 2015